Bittersweet

I could not have made it through this journey without
the unwavering love and support of my husband, Wiley.
Thank you for keeping my spirits lifted with your positivity
and humor during this life changing experience. I love you.

I dedicate this book to my family and friends taken by cancer;
Carol P. Bishop, Jimmy F. Britten, Rita V. Koeller, Katie Sue Kosmala,
Danielle Martin, Julianne Ward Nelson, Jessi Ray and Andrea Reno.

Contents

Introduction

Writing this book was unplanned, just like my diagnosis with cancer, but somehow once the idea had been planted, it made perfect sense. Never in a million years did I ever envision exposing photographs of my breasts to the world. All of the photos during my treatment were taken by my husband, Wiley, for our own record. We simply wanted to document the journey to be able to celebrate where I ended up afterwards. When I was going through the different phases of cancer, treatment, and reconstruction, I searched online but I could only find before and after photos. I wanted to know what happened in between, and I believed I wasn't the only one.

I realized that there were other women with breast cancer that wanted to see what was going to happen to their breasts after a mastectomy and through the process of reconstruction. I started to organize my photos and began to write. Reliving the whole awful experience again wasn't easy. Some days I cried my way through the details to write *Bittersweet*. The more I wrote, the more motivated I became to demystify what happens to a woman's breasts during breast cancer. Detailing each phase and photograph of what I endured was cathartic, I was healing my own trauma with each word I wrote.

Every women's experience with breast cancer is different. I am sharing what happened to me and hope that it helps to support you or someone you know. I don't give you every scenario or detail all of the medical options available. This is my story and I am sharing what I know as a result of my own breast cancer. I hope this book finds its way into the hands of those women that need the support. Share a copy with your mother, sister, and friends. We all know someone with breast cancer.

This book is not a substitute for professional medical care. Do not use this book as an alternative to a consultation with your physician. Only a qualified medical professional can evaluate your case and recommend treatment. I have made every effort to make sure that at the time of publication the information is accurate. However, new findings and recommendations may invalidate some of what has been presented. For the most accurate information, always consult your healthcare professionals.

Holly K. Thrasher

Chapter One
Candy Makes Life Sweeter

I stared at the two silicone mounds that had not yet completely healed from the effects of a two-year breast cancer drama, and wondered how I got here. In my mid-forties, I had rediscovered my long-lost childhood dream to open a nostalgic candy store and followed it. I was happy, fulfilled, and content until my breasts, body, and childhood dreams had been forced to change in the blink of an eye.

Before I was born, my dad, John K. Bishop, was an elementary school teacher in Orcutt, California. His wife, Carol P. Bishop, a secretary. They were living in a modest apartment and working the American dream but my dad was not satisfied, he wanted something more. He had graduated from Long Beach University with the goal of becoming a school teacher. A few years after he began his teaching career, he realized that teaching elementary aged children was not his calling and he hated it with a passion.

My dad contacted Mr. Bell about a new Taco Bell franchise he had heard about in Los Angeles. It was 1965 and my dad had no restaurant experience to speak of but after meeting Mr. Bell, both my parents agreed they had to buy their first Taco Bell franchise. They took all of their savings and ignored warnings from family members and moved ahead with their plan. My dad quit his teaching job and built his first Taco Bell on Milpas Street in Santa Barbara. It opened in 1966 when my mom was expecting her first child, my older sister, June.

My parents grew their family to three daughters and their Taco Bell business into a multi-million-dollar empire. They had a chain of twelve Taco Bells in California, from Santa Barbara to Bakersfield. My dad almost never took a day off. He loved his businesses and he was focused on giving my mom, myself, and my two sisters an incredible life. My dad's hard work provided us amazing opportunities, a private school education, and foreign travel. We had multiple Mercedes Benz in the driveway and my dads' general manager and wife drove them too. My mom had a convertible silver shadow Rolls Royce she drove only on Sundays and my dad had a vintage Jaguar XKE convertible roadster that he would race up and down our street just for fun.

I remember my dad always smelled of Crabtree & Evelyn jojoba soap, not the regular size bar, the bar shaped like a seashell. He always wore a long-sleeved button-down dress shirt monogrammed with his initials, JKB, on his right sleeve. He wore tailored pants and four-hundred-dollar leather shoes. He always looked like he was ready to meet someone new, first impressions were important to him. His very balding head was always covered by an expensive Stetson hat or one that he had custom made in a small hat shop in San Francisco that he had frequented for decades. He never skimped on quality. When it came to his restaurants, clothing, cars, or homes, he always purchased the best, reminding us girls, "You get what you pay for."

My mom was gracious, soft, and warm to everyone she met. She laughed lightly at all of my dad's jokes and adored him and his intellect. When he spoke, her eyes showed the deep love and respect that she had for him. She was always dressed elegantly, like my dad. It wasn't unusual to find her pruning in the garden or dragging a hose around while wearing a high-end designer silk blouse, tailored slacks in the best fabric, and her favorite Salvatore Ferragamo conservatively healed dress shoes. Her diamond and emerald wedding ring purchased at Cartier in New York City in the 1980's for their anniversary, sparkled under the water dripping from the hose. I always looked forward to her right hand gently rubbing my back as I talked to her about school or friends. Everyone that met her, loved her and she and my dad were always very generous to their employees, family, and our friends. My sisters and I learned from a young age that everything we had was a result of our parent's hard work.

Both of my parents loved early American and English one-of-a-kind antiques and every room of our sprawling home was filled with the pieces. They also loved old clocks. Table clocks, wall clocks, and grandfather clocks of every size and shape adorned our home. Every hour, the orchestra of chimes from each clock echoed through the rooms and sounded like we were living in a different era. My dad spent time every week making the rounds winding the clocks with old, brass keys. It was reminiscent of their favorite Masterpiece Theater television show *Upstairs, Downstairs*, a social, political, and historical drama that was set in Edwardian London. My parents modeled their home after that era of English nobility. Lord and Lady Bishop loved their fine country home decorated with rare, burled woods, delicate crystal glassware, and all of the noble trappings of their elegant life.

We lived at Midwood, a sprawling 7,500 square foot home in Montecito, California. Midwood was designed by famed architect Reginald Johnson in 1919. It was commissioned to be designed with elegant spaces that evoked a regal mood, but was comfortable and livable. It had the feeling of yesteryear but was thoroughly modern.

We had a staff, a private plane, a fulltime pilot, and everything we could possibly ever want. We were encouraged to work from an early age even though we lived a privileged life. At my first job at the age of twelve, I filled soft drinks in an excessively hot Bakersfield Taco Bell, while sweat dripped down my back. We loved to make our own food and drinks on the line when business was slow. My older sister and I took turns traveling to Bakersfield with our dad, when school permitted, and we worked long hours by his side. Our custom made, brown and orange polyester uniforms matched those of our fellow co-workers and we were treated as their equals, but it was clear to all that we were the boss' daughters. We worked open to close for days at a time and we loved it. My dad thought it was important to teach us the value of work and money, so, he paid us $8.00 an hour with cash that was carefully counted out of his personal money clip. That was a lot of money back then, but he wanted us to be motivated.

I remember hearing my dad instruct his employees to "Flip, whip, stir, the meat, beans and sauces." It was a phrase that was drilled into the employees to make sure that the food was the very best it could be. At the time, everything was made fresh in the kitchens of our Taco Bells. Blocks of cheese were grated fresh daily. The sauces were made from scratch and the meat cooked and seasoned to perfection. The food was amazing. It was one of the reasons that year after year, my dad's franchises were praised by the corporate offices and his bank accounts flush with cash.

I would be exhausted by the end of my work day and would fall into bed around midnight each night. The next day, I put my uniform back on, and went back to work. My dad included us in his business meetings and introduced us to his food vendors as part of our business education. As a result, I knew as a child that someday I would own my own business.

My dad was very proud of us girls, and if he ever longed-for boys, I never felt it. He loved to introduce the Bishop Girls in order of our birth, June was the oldest, I was the middle daughter, Holly, and the youngest was my sister, Sarah. We were all born two years apart in the months of April and May and all five of us celebrated our birthdays in those same two months. I always felt like my dad's favorite daughter when I was with him. I'm sure he did that for each of my sisters too, as he was kind, loving, and we all adored him. When we complained about anything, he would tell us, "Life isn't fair, get used to it." Looking back, it was rather ironic considering we were living a privileged life and most everything in our lives was more than fair.

Our home was popular with our friends and they came home with us after school on Fridays and stayed over until Sunday evening when their parents forced them back home to prepare for school on Monday. My parents never seemed bothered by all of the chaos multiple teenage girls created and it wasn't unusual to have at least six girls in the house every weekend. I had been attending Laguna Blanca School since Kindergarten and longed to follow my friends to public school. At the age of sixteen, I begged my parents to let me leave private school and go to Santa Barbara High School for Junior year.

After I got my way, I found myself in the large halls of the high school with students from every walk of life. I floundered outside the small bubble I had spent most of my life in at private school. I wouldn't realize it for many years but that move to SBHS was one that would transform my whole life. It was 1986, and I watched giggling teenage girls pass notes across each desk during fourth period math at SBHS. The carefully folded and concealed notes arrived in the hands of a young man with a soft smile and slicked back dark hair sitting across the room from me. He appeared to be pretty popular with almost everyone and seemed so friendly. I had met him a few days earlier in Mrs. Taylor's first period art class.

His name was Wiley Dean Thrasher and I wanted to be his friend. I loved his black leather jacket, the way he safety pinned his black jeans so they were tapered at the bottom and how independent he was, riding to and from school on a white Yamaha scooter. It took a few days to decide to pass him a note and soon I was holding a note back from him inviting me to his friend Jeff's house for a party that weekend.

Wiley and I became best friends and spent all of our time together during high school and into our college years. That close friendship slowly developed into love and we surprised our family and friends when we started dating, August 22, 1990, almost five years after meeting. We were 21 years old and we realized we didn't want to be apart.

We married in 1994 at the Rockwood Woman's Club in Santa Barbara. My parents, John and Carol, hosted the black-tie wedding. Wiley and I modeled our marriage after my parents' as it was obvious to everyone that John and Carol were a great team and we were too. My parents always encouraged us girls to try new things and not to limit ourselves. After working for my dad for years in the restaurant business, I branched out and found a love for retail. I assumed that one day I would quit retail and my dad and I would open a restaurant together.

In the late 1980's, a large corporation purchased the Taco Bell brand and announced they were eliminating the kitchens in all of the restaurants. Food quality was the most important aspect of owning and operating a restaurant for my dad and without a kitchen, he was no longer interested in owning his Taco Bells. He sold off his entire chain of restaurants and pursued new business ideas. My family continued to work and support my dad's numerous restaurants as we grew into adults, the most notable being The Good Earth Restaurant in Goleta and his last business, Go Taco in San Luis Obispo. Without the large income from the Taco Bells, my parents slowly drained their accounts living off of their savings. They didn't bother to alter their lifestyle as they believed the next big thing was right around the corner. My dad had always been successful in all of his business efforts, so they carried on as if nothing had changed.

My dad sunk the last of the cash he received from the sale of the Taco Bells into numerous businesses including a pizza chain. The sellers gave my dad inaccurate financial information that made the businesses look more profitable than they were. The businesses failed within the first year after my dad tried to right them. That huge mistake plunged them into bankruptcy. My sisters and I were happily married off, so my parents moved out of Santa Barbara to protect themselves from the disappointment and embarrassment of bankruptcy. They landed a few hours up the coast in San Luis Obispo and my dad found the old Taco Bell building my uncle had built in the 1970's was for lease. My dad longed for his taco stand years and wanted to go back to that original dream. My parents had no money after the bankruptcy and my dad felt hopeless and depressed about their future.

My mom phoned me and asked if I would talk to my dad, as she was worried about him. It was an unusual request coming from my mom. She usually acted like everything was always alright. I knew he must really need it. I phoned my dad and gave him a pep-talk. I told him that I knew he could do it and that he needed to find a way to make his taco stand dream happen. His close friend and fellow restauranteur, Roger Duncan, owned and operated the successful Rusty's Pizza chain in Santa Barbara. He had known my dad for decades and knew his work ethic, so, he offered the money needed for my dad to once again go back into the taco business almost 30 years later. Six months after bankruptcy, my dad leased my uncle's original Taco Bell building. It was a proud moment for our family when the doors opened to Go Taco. My dad modeled it after the original recipes and quality food he knew and loved.

I was nearing my thirtieth birthday and I began to question what I should be doing with my career. It was the Summer of 1999 and I had phoned my dad to ask him what he thought of a local cheesecake business that was for sale in Santa Barbara. I considered buying it and thought he might even want to go into business with me. I was shocked by what he said to me that day. He told me, "The restaurant business is too hard and too many hours, Holly, you need to do something else." *How could he be telling me to do something else when he had worked his entire life in the food industry and made a tremendous success of it?* It made no sense. I argued cheesecake wasn't a restaurant but he explained that it was food service and nearly the same thing. "Promise me you won't go into the restaurant business," he said.

He was adamant that I make the promise. My dad had never asked anything that serious of me, so I promised my dad that I would never go into the restaurant business. I assumed that one day he would change his mind and I thought nothing more of it. It was late in the afternoon when we spoke and I didn't think much of the strangeness of that conversation. It was the last conversation we ever had.

My dad would usually be home with my mom in the evening with his feet up on an ottoman reading The Wall Street Journal after a long day at the taco stand. That night, June 15, 1999 was different. The Go Taco manager had phoned in sick, leaving only my dad to close the store on such short notice. My mom insisted on going with him since it was approaching midnight. She was in the office at the back of the restaurant counting the money from the day, when she heard a loud crashing sound. She ran to my dad's side. His body lay lifeless on the black rubber restaurant mats, his glasses broken when they were knocked off his head in the fall. Blood was on his face, his glasses, and the stainless restaurant counter where hours earlier, employees bustled about stuffing taco shells with homemade seasoned meat for hungry customers.

The phone woke Wiley and I up just after one in the morning. In a shallow, emotionless voice, my mom told me that my dad had died of a heart attack. She was in shock. The pain was suffocating, but I kept my cool and offered to help my mom by calling my youngest sister, Sarah, for her. My mom had phoned us in order of our birth, just like our dad used to introduce us. My oldest sister, June, had already endured receiving the shocking news. I could tell by my mom's voice she was near the point of being unable to speak further. Just then, my dad's brother, my uncle David, arrived at the hospital with his wife Karen to drive her home. I hung up the phone and sobbed uncontrollably in Wiley's arms. My world was forever changed knowing that my dad was gone forever.

I took a deep breath and phoned Sarah. She knew something was wrong immediately as I didn't make it a habit of waking her up in the middle of the night. She started to panic sensing the devastation in my voice and our new reality. My younger sister screamed in anguish on the other end of the phone as I told her our dad was gone. The only thing that brought me any sense of relief was knowing that I had told him that I loved him before I had hung up the phone that same day. Life always felt safe with my dad in it, but he was suddenly gone and my mom was all alone and it felt like my sisters and I were too. When I woke up the next morning, the conversation my dad and I had the day before, the day of his death, haunted me. *Did he somehow unconsciously know that he was going to die? Why had I promised something so important on his dying day?* He was a man of his word and I wanted to be just like him. Even though I had been well educated in the restaurant business and always assumed I would ultimately run a restaurant, I knew I never would. I continued to work in retail, fulfilling other people's dreams.

Ten years after I made that promise, I was turning 40 years old and ready to open my own business. Wiley and I had a son, Vance, and he was entering first grade. It was the perfect time for me to open my own business. The problem was, I had no idea what kind of business to open. I didn't want to own a clothing store or a gift shop and I was not opening a restaurant. I racked my brain for months for an idea that would work in the small town we called home, Ojai, California.

One evening after dinner, Vance and I were watching an episode of the TV show, *Unwrapped*, on the Food Network. The episode was called "Candy Cravings" and the host, Marc Summers, was introducing us to the world of candy. He was touring candy factories and sweet shops, and attending the Sweets and Snacks Expo in Chicago. I was enthralled with this new world I knew nothing about. Then it hit me. I jumped off the sofa, thrust my arms in the air and yelled, "I'm going to open a candy store!" Vance was nine years old at the time and loved the idea. He jumped around the living room yelling, "Yes!" I ran into Wiley's home office where he was still working into the evening, reminiscent of my dad's dedication. It was a light bulb moment I could not ignore and Wiley, agreed.

Sure, candy was something you ate, but I never intended to make any candy and it was not the restaurant business, so I felt that my promise to my dad was being honored. My dad had had quite a sweet tooth and he used to hide boxes of See's candy in cupboards and drawers at his house. I knew he would have loved it. The rest of my extended family were in full support and I became obsessed with the world of candy.

It wasn't until I started researching the candy business that I came across photos of me as a young girl in my childhood candy store. My candy store was set up in the closet under our staircase at our first home in Montecito. It was the home we lived in before we moved to Midwood. My parents had purchased the home from author Fannie Flagg, best known for her book turned movie, *Fried Green Tomatoes*, and actress, Susan Flannery, who had a role on the soap opera, *The Bold and the Beautiful*. Fannie and Susan had left my sisters and I a vintage, red, metal bubble gum machine as a gift when we moved into our new home. Like many adults, I had forgotten my childhood dream, the candy store under the stairs, and that red bubble gum machine. They had disappeared from my memory but my passion for candy stores was reignited. It felt like I had found my destiny and I had no doubts it would be a success.

It was 2009, and the economy had not recovered from the financial crisis many economists proclaimed was the worst since the great depression. Many people told me it was the worst time to open a small business and that we would lose everything, a fear that was very valid after watching my parents lose their home, business, financial security, and pride. Those warnings, however, did nothing to deter me. I felt the exact opposite. It seemed like the perfect time to open a candy store. A nostalgic candy store would remind people of their childhoods and would be a joyful diversion from the scary economic reality that plagued many. The candy store would be a fun place to create new memories and it could fit into just about everyone's budget.

I had been managing a retail store in Ojai for two years after being a stay-at-home mom to Vance for the first eight years of his life. Discovering my dream again was all I could think about and I ignored the warnings and gave my two-week notice at work that same week. I created a business plan and mapped out all of the candy stores within a three-hour radius. My dad never went into a new business without proper research and a plan. I started my candy store field trips to check out the competition and complete my research. My new adventure had begun.

We decided on the name, Kingston's Candy Co., named for my dad, John Kingston Bishop, and our son, Vance Kingston Thrasher. Kingston was a family name and our dad had insisted that all three of his girl's middle names start with a K, a nod to his middle name and father's family. Armed with an idea, a business name, and a growing passion for the candy industry, we took out a small loan against some money that had been left to me by my maternal grandmother, Rita, a devout Christian Scientist and one of my biggest cheerleaders in life. We opened Kingston's Candy Co. on March 19th, 2010. Located on the main street in Ojai, Kingston's quickly became a popular hang-out for all ages. *Who could resist being a kid in a candy store?* It was a sweet business and I had found my calling owning my own business and being known as the local candy lady.

In May 2010, two months after opening Kingston's, I was supposed to fly to The Candy Expo in Chicago with my sister June. My sister had a serious and unexpected illness that hospitalized her and Wiley was unable to go because of his job. I almost cancelled, but the expo was a dream of mine and I was excited for the adventure, even if I had to go by myself. Upon arriving at the Expo on the first day, to my complete surprise and delight, I discovered that Marc Summers was speaking at the Expo. It was a full circle moment for me, meeting the man that had set off my adventure into the very sweet world of candy after I watched his popular television show *Unwrapped*. After Marc spoke to a very crowded room of admirers, I rushed to speak with him as the line queued up behind me. I only had a few minutes with him and I quickly shared my story with Marc and took a photo with him. Life was sweet. Everything was falling into place.

Over the six years we were in business, I had the opportunity to hire many young, first time employees. Employees gave me a little bit more freedom, since I was also a wife and mom. We became very close to some of our employees and we considered them part of our family. We started to refer to them as our "adopted daughters without all of the paperwork". Chelsi, Hannah, Nicole, Jordan, Alexis, Lucia and others came into our lives as employees and made Kingston's a success and ultimately became family. They would help us through not one but two medical dramas.

One year after opening Kingston's, I suffered several TIA's, transient ischemic attacks, also known as mini-strokes. I had suffered from migraine with aura headaches and a list of other symptoms since I was a child but never knew their cause due to my Christian Science upbringing. At the age of 42, I was diagnosed with a very large PFO, patent foramen ovale, a hole in the wall of the upper chambers (atria) of my heart. I had been born with it, but it wasn't until I was in my 40's that it gave me real problems. I had no idea that 25% of the adult population had a PFO. The majority of people never had any symptoms, but I was part of the very small group of patients that experienced major symptoms.

I dealt with low blood oxygen levels, dizziness, shortness of breath, migraines, and it got worse weekly. My doctor ordered me an oxygen tank and I was using it 24 hours a day. The first day on oxygen at Kingston's, several customers walked in, took a look at the cannula on my face, then turned and bolted out. My "happy place" was being affected by my health and from then on, I monitored my oxygen levels with a pulse oximeter on my finger. When my oxygen levels dropped, I hid in my office sucked in oxygen from my tank until my levels went back to normal. I would watch the security cameras from the office and return to the front of the store when customers entered. It was a stressful time. I remained working in my business and kept it a happy place for customers. I had an oxygen tank for six challenging months before my medical insurance agreed to fix my heart.

I was referred to UCLA cardiologist, Dr. Jonathon Tobis who had decades of experience with my type of issue and agreed to close the hole in my heart on April 11, 2013. A Gore-Helix septal occluder device was put into my heart using a trans-catheter procedure. The umbrella shaped device would literally plug the hole between my left and right ventricle. The trans-catheter procedure on my heart was considered pretty standard. It always seemed strange to me that putting a device into something as vital as a human heart was considered, no big deal.

My cardiologist proved his talent, by checking me in at seven in the morning, fixing my heart in a two-hour procedure, and then sending me on my way by five in the evening. Crazy as it sounds, I was on the 405 freeway in Los Angeles, heading home to Ojai the very same day. The device almost immediately resolved all of my symptoms. I took eight days off from the candy store to heal from the procedure and then jumped right back into work. My heart was fixed and I felt like I had just experienced my "one big thing." I was convinced that the rest of my forties would be smooth sailing. *Ha, I was so wrong.*

In 2014, I opened our private label wholesale business, *Candy Makes Life Sweeter*. I was running the retail store and designing private label candy for other businesses. I had a sales rep selling my candy to retail stores up and down the California coast. I was proud to call The Madonna Inn in San Luis Obispo and The Ojai Valley Inn and Spa some of my two dozen clients. I was working a lot of hours managing those two candy businesses, but it felt like I was living my dream. I could not imagine doing anything else. Plus, I was finally making money after six years in business. From 2010 to 2016, Kingston's, brought me so much joy. Life was good, business was good, and I felt I had found my calling.

Holly posing in Kingston's Candy Co. Life was sweet.

Holly showing off her profits in her very first candy store under the stairs in Montecito, early 1980's.

Meeting Marc Summers, Chicago, May 2010. Holly dressed up as a Kingston's Candy Girl for an event.

Vance, Holly and Wiley Celebrating Kingston's Five-Year Anniversary, March 2015.
Hannah, Holly, and Chelsi dressed up as Kingston's Candy Girls, March 2014.

Ojai Valley Chamber of Commerce Small Business of the Year 2011.
Holly, Jordan, Nicole and Chelsi all smiles working at Kingston's.

Chapter Two
Breast Cancer Journey Begins
November 2015

My parents, John and Carol, were just teenagers when they met at a Christian Science youth group in the 1950's. They were both being raised by devoted Christian Science mothers and attended church regularly. They became friends as teenagers but lost touch after high school. A mutual friend re-introduced them, they fell in love, and married in 1961. They continued to practice their religion together as a couple. As I was growing up, I remember them each with their leather-bound copy of Science and Health with Keys to the Scriptures by Mary Baker Eddy. It was the guide book for Christian Scientists. They would read their weekly lesson and use blue chalk pens to highlight the most important passages. They were devoted students developing their intricate web of prayer, positive thinking, and denial.

We were expected to attend Sunday School at the Christian Science Church in Santa Barbara every Sunday with my parents. As we learned lessons in prayer and were gently guided toward the idea that sickness and disease did not exist, those ideas were challenged over the years by regular sleepovers at the Gordin's house. Dr. David Gordin was an orthopedic surgeon and father of four; Suzy, David, Andrea and Stacy. His wife, Marianne, was a stunning Italian woman with dark hair and eyes, olive skin and a radiant smile. Marianne was a nurse and took care of her family and everyone else's too. There were always a lot of kids at the house and Marianne served us meals from huge pots of pasta in her gourmet kitchen. My sisters and I each had a Gordin in our grade at school and we all became close friends.

I remember meeting Andrea Gordin for the first time in Kindergarten at Laguna Blanca School, the private day school we all attended. One Saturday morning, I woke up at the Gordin's after a fun sleepover with a terrible sore throat. I was supposed to stay another night and didn't want to go home early. I told Dr. Gordin I felt sick and my throat really hurt. He took a look at my throat and opened the medicine cupboard in Marianne's kitchen. He instructed me to open my mouth and he sprayed a red, cherry flavored concoction into the back of my throat. My throat immediately felt better and I was able to run back out into their yard to play and continued my sleepover. There was no cupboard at my house with any type of medicines. The most we had were band aids and we never had a can of antiseptic spray that all the other moms generously sprayed on open wounds.

We also never had a television growing up, so we created ways to live without it. Stacy and Andrea spent the weekend at our house quite frequently and on that particular weekend, we laced up our roller skates and hit the driveway. Someone got the brilliant idea that we should leash our two hyper Dalmatian dogs, Becky and Falstaff, and let them pull us up and down the street at break neck speed. It all started out innocently enough until Stacy took a fall that put an end to the fun.

Stacy went down hard when the leashes crossed each other and tangled up, her well-worn, 1970's style roller skates came out from under her and she landed on her side on the hard, black asphalt. Stacy gripped her arm to her chest as tears streamed down her face. Stacy almost never cried, so we knew it must be serious. We helped Stacy into the house and alerted our mom to her injury.

My mom assessed the situation and told Stacy that she was just fine. Stacy put on a brave face, but by evening, she was crying again and wanted to talk to her dad. Stacy phoned her dad and told him what had happened, but my mom had already spoken to the experienced orthopedic surgeon, and planted the seed of doubt in him that anything was wrong with her arm. Stacy was denied an early ride home and basically told to "suck it up."

As we all prepared for bed that night we felt pretty upset for Stacy. In the middle of the night, we woke up to find her sobbing. My sister Sarah and I woke my parents and told them in no uncertain terms, that Stacy's arm was broken and she needed to go home. Dr. Gordin arrived early that morning and felt her arm from wrist to shoulder, proclaiming that it was indeed broken. I felt a mix of anger and confusion as to why Stacy was forced to endure a broken arm for more than half a day before her dad reset the bone and put a cast on it. The lessons that I heard at church on Sunday mornings that taught me that a broken arm was not real, began to make no sense to me. A broken arm was real and I had witnessed it. My mom expressed regret over Stacy's broken arm but never admitted that it was indeed broken.

I began to question everything that I had been taught and I began to form the opinion that Christian Science was wrong to deny medical treatment and replace it with prayer. As I had more and more experiences with actual illnesses of my own and saw others healed with medicines and doctor visits, my religious rebellion continued to grow. *Why were other kids getting the attention they deserved when injured? Why were we being trained to ignore our illnesses and pretend our symptoms didn't exist?*

We had loving and involved Christian Science parents, but once I reached my teenage years, I did not identify with the ideas that were being taught. I never thought of myself as a practicing Christian Scientist and once out of the house, I never pursued the religion. Both my sisters, June and Sarah, felt the same as I did about the religion. Although we tried to respect our parents' beliefs, it was not always easy. There was a voice deep inside me that would not let me practice the religion, an intimate knowing, that it was not right for me and that it would not end well for any of us if we stuck to that belief system. That questioning voice inside me was right, and it cost my parent's their lives far too early.

My dad's sudden death in 1999 came as a surprise. We had been conditioned to be positive and never thought about the worst-case scenario. He had ignored his high blood pressure and heart condition for years, and continued to work in the high stress restaurant industry. It was obvious that my dad was at risk but we had been trained to never entertain that idea. His unexpected death took a toll on my mom as they had spent the last forty years together.

Three years after his death, just as the fog of grief started to lift and joy was back in our lives, my sisters and I sat at our mom's bedside as she took her last death rattled breath. She had died of cancer, most likely breast cancer from the symptoms, but we would never know for sure as my mom had refused all medical intervention. She died in a Christian Science facility in Pasadena and we never asked for an autopsy as we had agreed to honor her beliefs and wishes.

Losing both parents in my early 30's only three years apart felt like a boulder had rolled down a mountain and rested on my chest. Vance was a happy go lucky eighteenth month old at the time and I had one foot in the world of grief and the other in the land of the living. I was resolved that I would never let that happen to me. I took a proactive approach toward my health and I was not going to practice prayer as my parents had. Old habits are hard to break, especially the ones that you are not even aware of.

In January of 2014, an old friend from high school, Andrea, lost her battle with breast cancer. The very next month, a second, high school friend, Julianne, also lost her life from breast cancer. *How could this happen?* Both woman, in their 40's were loving mothers, wives, and friends. They were just like me. They had everything to live for. They both left behind young children and devastated husbands. It felt surreal and totally unfair. Even though we had not seen each other in person for years, we had been following each other's lives through social media. Their deaths hit me hard. I felt an overwhelming sense of loss, as if the rug had once again been pulled out from under me. I could hear my dad say, "Life isn't fair," and in the back of my mind, I knew it wasn't. I made an appointment for a mammogram that month to honor both of their deaths and to put my mind at ease. If it could happen to them, it could happen to me.

I had always thought of myself as proactive, opposite of what my parents had chosen for themselves. Every month I saw a lymphatic therapist because there was more than one spot on both breasts that was intermittently sore. I was sure that the small lump just to the right and below my left nipple was just a cyst. Every year I had a breast thermography and every year the results came back normal. Nothing to worry about. Out of an abundance of caution, I got a baseline mammogram in 2004 at the age of 35 to compare against any future mammograms.

In 2009, I had a second mammogram which was miserable. The pressure of the mammogram caused a thick yellow fluid to be expelled out of my left nipple. The nurse doing the mammogram questioned if I had ever had any kind of discharge before. I told her that I hadn't, but she didn't seem concerned about it. I was told it was most likely a cyst that burst. It was incredibly sore that evening and I spent several days icing what felt like internal bruising. After that experience, I had sworn off any future mammograms, but fear was a very powerful motivator. To honor my friends, I got past that fear and made an appointment for a mammogram. It was February 2014 and my latest mammogram results came back with "suspicious findings" in my left breast. They had compared the new mammogram to my previous two and recommended an ultrasound guided biopsy. I was told not to worry as "85% of these are benign and not cancerous."

My doctor followed up the mammogram with an ultrasound which confirmed that I had a "clinically suspicious palpable lump" that needed to be biopsied. The ultrasound tech said she could squeeze me into their schedule that same week. I heard what she said but told myself that everything was fine and I refused the biopsy. I was able to justify my decision because it had not even been a year since I had the PFO (hole in my heart) fixed and I was still waiting to be cleared by my cardiologist. I thought there was nothing to worry about because that was what I had been told for years. I had convinced myself that my heart drama was my one big thing. There was just no way I had breast cancer. I ignored the medical advice and went on with my sweet life.

I was quite comfortable ignoring the truth as I had been trained as a child to believe illness was not real, it was error. Even though I didn't practice Christian Science, its doctrine had seeped into my unconscious and was hiding there. I was taught for years that any pain or discomfort was to be prayed away. If it didn't go away, you must not be praying hard enough. If we were really sick as kids my mom would call in a Christian Science practitioner to help guide our thoughts and to reinforce positive thinking. Prayer and positive thought were the cornerstone of the religion and you could not be happy and healthy without it. We were taught to ignore the way we felt and our own intuition. That denial became a very effective coping mechanism and was impacting my adult decision making when it came to the suspicious lump in my breast.

I was at my annual exam in October 2015, one year and eight months after my last mammogram resulted in "suspicious findings". My doctor said that she was very concerned that I had ignored the lump in my breast and had not followed up with the results of my last mammogram. My one big thing was over and I had been cleared by my cardiologist. I saw that I had pretended that everything was fine and that had been a very bad idea. The lump had not gone away and it actually felt bigger. I was ready to cope with the breast lump and face reality. It was November 2015 and I agreed to another ultrasound, another mammogram, and I scheduled the ultrasound guided biopsy.

Less than a week later, I stopped into my primary care physician's office to inquire if my breast biopsy test results had been returned. The young and brand new, front desk receptionist took a look in her computer and confirmed that they were back. She asked if I would like a copy. Waiting for test results was excruciating. I figured that it must be good news if she was handing me a copy and wishing me a good day.

I sat in my car in the parking lot at my doctor's office and pulled out the report. I read all the way down to the part that read; "The pathology report is now available and shows malignancy concordant with the findings. Pathology report positive for infiltrating ductal adenocarcinoma." *Wait, what? Malignancy? Carcinoma?* Carcinoma was cancer, I thought. I sat in my car for a while just trying to digest the gravity of those words. Then I started to yell, "What the Fuck? Fuck! Seriously, I have breast cancer and I'm finding out all alone in my car?"

I got out of my car and went back into my doctor's office. I knocked on the glass window that separated the receptionist and myself. The receptionist that had kindly just handed me the results, smiled and said, "Can I help you?" I explained that I needed to speak with someone right away because the results of my biopsy were not good. She looked a little freaked out, I think I was acting a little freaked out too. She ran into the back of the office and within seconds, the door to the treatment area opened and the nurse called my name. She grabbed me and gave me a big hug. She apologized profusely and ushered me into a private room. I felt numb. I just needed someone to explain what I needed to do next. One of the doctors entered the room and spoke to me. I have no idea who it was or how that conversation went. None. She was horrified that my test results had been handed through the glass window without any hesitation and without a doctor there to explain what they meant. I was the last patient in that office to get bad news alone because they tightened their test result protocol. A doctor had to be consulted from then on, so that test results would not be handed out willy-nilly.

After I broke the news to Wiley that we had a new challenge ahead of us, I told him that I wanted to close both candy businesses. It had only been hours since my diagnosis, but I had a very strong sense of clarity when it came to my health and work. I knew that cancer was going to demand my full attention and require a whole lot more than my heart drama and the eight days I took off work to fix that. Breast cancer had killed some of my friends and most likely my own mom. My aunt, my mother's sister, had a rare, aggressive kind of breast cancer and I knew that it might be deadly for me.

I reflected on the lessons I had been taught and how both parents had decided at young ages to live their lives without any medical intervention. That lack of medical intervention took both parents away from my sisters and I when we had young families and needed grandparents for our children and mentors for ourselves. I chose to treat my breast cancer using all of the latest medical treatments available to me. I never wanted Vance to question whether I had done enough to save my own life and continue to live for his. Wiley agreed with me and we started to make medical decisions together after asking lots of questions and doing lots of research.

Diagnosed in November, right before the holidays, we kept the businesses open through the busiest season of the year and we planned to close our doors in January 2016. It might sound weird but the timing of my cancer and closing the store was perfect. My childhood dream had been realized and it had been very well received and loved by our special town of Ojai for six whole years. Thankfully, our lease was up in February and closing the store would be easier than I anticipated.

Ojai was such a small town and I knew Kingston's closing would impact my customers and those that knew me, so I decided I would not hide my illness. I would share my cancer journey with anyone and everyone that wanted to listen. I posted my new reality on my personal and business Facebook pages, I was interviewed for our local newspaper, the Ojai Valley News, and I shared my new reality with my loyal customers when they came into the store.

I needed help, I asked for it, and it started to pour in. Notes, cards, flowers, gifts, and messages of healing came from those close to me and people I had never even met. I knew that I had done the right thing. I was sharing a difficult experience and those around me stepped up to support not only myself but my husband, my teenage son, and our business when we needed it the most. It was such a huge lesson in love and community.

Wiley's job of almost two decades at Hewlett Packard provided us with decent medical insurance and I was able to secure appointments with both a female oncologist and surgeon in our area. I had been diagnosed with the most common type of breast cancer, 80% of all breast cancers are infiltrating ductal adenocarcinoma, also known as Invasive Ductal Carcinoma (IDC). Invasive means that the cancer had spread or invaded the surrounding breast tissue. There are many different types of breast cancer and I remember my oncologist saying, "This is the one you want."

Even though I had ignored the lump in my breast for as long as I did, I had still caught it in the early stages. My lump, was now being called a tumor. It was almost double the size it had been in the first mammogram and was considered T2 because of its size. My cancer cells were ER+ (positive), PR+ (positive), HER2- (negative). ER+ meant that my cancer cells were growing in response to the hormone estrogen. PR+ meant that my cancer cells were also growing in response to the hormone progesterone. HER2- meant the protein sometimes found on the surface of breast cancer cells was not present. Reducing or eliminating the hormones estrogen and progesterone were going to be a priority in my treatment and to further prevent cancer.

My surgeon, Dr. Constanze Rayhrer came highly recommended. I had so many questions about my diagnosis and what my treatment options were. I was told that my cancer cells were very aggressive, however, we could choose to go with a lumpectomy or single mastectomy. She did note that the chances of reoccurrence within five years in the other breast was high. Doctors will not make the decision for you. They will give you all the options and you have to decide on the treatment. Wiley and I conferred and immediately decided that a double mastectomy was the best option for long term survival. If the chances were high for cancer reoccurrence within five years, both breasts had to go. Dr. Rayhrer mentioned that she was relieved that we were taking the more aggressive approach. She suggested the surgery could be completed that week, but she gave me time to go home and make my decision. I didn't need any more time. I knew in my gut that they both needed to be removed.

We booked the surgery at that first consultation. I would be removing both breasts in two weeks; a bilateral total mastectomy with sentinel node dissection. That meant, both breasts and both nipples would be removed. Some women kept their nipples during a mastectomy, but in my case, the tumor was too close to it and the cancer cells too aggressive. It was safest to remove the nipple tissue as well. She would be doing a sentinel node dissection during the mastectomy to find out if the cancer had spread to my lymph nodes. She would remove at least one lymph node on each side and test them for cancer. If she found cancer in the first lymph node she would remove a second and so on until the lymph nodes were clear of cancer cells.

I liked my breasts. They fit my body and I was comfortable with them. After eight months of breast feeding and 46 years of gravity, they had lost their youthful perk, but they were mine and I was devastated to be losing them. I had never imagined myself with breast implants. Always the optimist, I decided not to dwell on how unfair it all was and I never questioned, "Why me?" That didn't seem relevant. *Why not me, knowing that 1 in 8 US women will be diagnosed with breast cancer in their lifetime?*

What was going to happen to my breasts? How would losing my breasts effect my feelings of self-worth and sexuality? What were they going to look like when they were removed? What did reconstruction, tissue expanders, and implant surgery look like? My breasts had been good to me, but they were just breasts and I didn't want to die of breast cancer, so they had to go. I turned to the internet for answers but found only before and after pictures. I needed more information. I wanted photos of what it looked like from beginning to end and everything in between, but couldn't find anything.

The week of my surgery, Wiley took photos of both breasts. They would be gone in five days and he was concerned that I might want to look back at them someday or share the photos with my plastic surgeon at a future appointment. That started our photographic journal. We took photos of every stage of my breast cancer treatment. I hadn't thought about ever sharing the photos with anyone other than medical professionals. It just seemed like a good idea at the time and I knew it would later help us both heal not only the physical cancer scars but the emotional as well.

We needed to be planning my future and believing that I was going to live. When things got tough, we said out loud in an authoritative voice, "We will rebuild!" It meant rebuilding both my breasts and my life. We had heard President Obama use the phrase in a speech, "We will rebuild, we will recover." It seemed a fitting motto for my situation.

28

Asking Santa (David Tate) to bring me new breasts for Christmas.

Getting a kiss from Wiley.

Kingston's Closing Day, January 10, 2016, four weeks after my double mastectomy.
Holly, Alexis, and Wiley take one last photo together in the store.
Close friend, Edward Prichard III, came to help make our last day in business a fun one.

John K. and Carol P. Bishop

Chapter Two: Practical Suggestions

- Do not ignore signs or symptoms that something physically is wrong. Denial will not benefit you in the long run.

- Choose your team of doctors and oncologists based on referrals and your consultation appointments.

- If you don't agree with what a doctor is telling you, get a second opinion.

- Switch doctors if you need to. Your life is on the line and you need to have someone you trust.

- Take a small notebook with you to every single appointment and take notes.

- If it is easier, you can record your appointments on your mobile phone.

- Before every doctor's appointment make a list of questions about your cancer, symptoms, treatment options, and chances of reoccurrence in your notebook.

- For some reason, it is not unusual to have your mind go completely blank while in your doctor's office, so be prepared.

- Follow your own intuition and push for answers to your questions.

- Follow up with further testing if it is needed.

- Start to build your support group. Ask friends and family for help. Do not feel guilty about asking.

- If friends and family are not in a position to help, be understanding and move on to those that can offer support.

- Don't feel bad about saying no to any invitations or requests for your presence. You have a lot on your plate, so do not commit yourself to any new obligations you don't want to do.

- Eat regular meals and try to get enough sleep.

- Meditate and exercise to relieve your stress and anxiety. Don't forget to breathe.

Chapter Three
Total Double Mastectomy
November 27, 2015

Wiley took our first set of breast photos five days before I was scheduled for my total double mastectomy. My left breast was puckered above my nipple from the tumor and the nipple on the left looked different from the right. I wasn't experiencing any pain or discomfort, just fear. The quote by renowned Swiss psychiatrist, Carl Jung, "What you resist, persists" reminded me to let go, and just allow it all to unfold. When I felt myself clinging or gripping to an idea or a fear, I gently reminded myself to let go and stop resisting. I did a lot of crying that week. I was scared to lose my life to breast cancer and also scared of such a major surgery as I was not experienced with it. The procedure to fix my heart was significant but nothing compared to both breasts removed. Nobody ever said breast cancer was going to be easy, but I was reassured that I had a very good chance of survival. So, I focused on the prize, my life.

I had never had any serious thoughts of changing my physical appearance with surgery and I wrestled with the whole idea of breast implants. *I never had a perfect body but who does?* It was my body, my breasts and I liked them, actually, I loved them. I didn't want them to be removed but I also realized that they were only breasts. I loved my life more. I saw a tank top online that said, "Yes, their fake. My real ones tried to kill me." That really resonated with me. Maybe, I needed my breasts to take responsibility for the pain and anguish they had caused me. If I blamed them it might make it a little easier to let them go.

Wiley held my hand and said, "I love you Holly. We know how to do this. Everything is going to be alright." I believed him. We smiled, laughed, and enjoyed the nervous time before the surgery. My body was about to change and I didn't fight it, I embraced it as much as one could when gripped with such uncertainty. I felt deep down that the double mastectomy was the right choice. I wanted the cancer gone and I wanted a longer life. *I didn't know then that cancer changes you. It changes your body and the way you look at the world. It alters the way you feel every night before you go to bed and the way you feel when you wake up every morning. Goodbye breasts. You were good to me, but you have to go.*

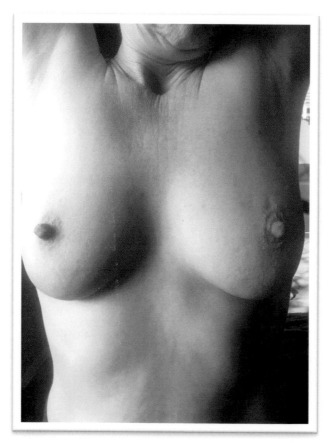

Puckering or dimpling of the skin, as seen on the top of my left breast, was a sign of my tumor.

Change
December 7, 2015

My nipples and most of my breast tissue were removed during the bilateral total mastectomy surgery on December 7th. It was my best friend, Rosalie's birthday and Pearl Harbor Day, memorable in more than one way. After my mastectomy was completed, Dr. Rayhrer performed a manual lymph node dissection on either side. She began by removing one lymph node from my right side under my arm pit. She tested that lymph node for cancer cells and when it came back clear she moved to my left side and removed three lymph nodes that also came back clear. The cancer had not spread on either side, so radiation treatment would not be needed.

My surgeon preserved as much breast tissue as possible, leaving me with a base to use during breast reconstruction. There were hidden sutures along with the glue to hold the incisions closed. I also had very small incisions on either side of my breasts where the temporary drains were inserted. Drains were necessary to clear out excess blood and lymph that would accumulate in the area after surgery. The drains were removed about one week later when the amount of fluid had substantially decreased.

I will never forget the look on Wiley's face as Dr. Rayhrer removed the drains. We both had assumed that there was an inch or two of tubing in my chest. We were so wrong. Wiley had offered to remove the drains at home the night before since they were no longer draining, but I told him that I wanted to wait for the doctor to remove them. He said it was no big deal and he could do it easily. Ha.

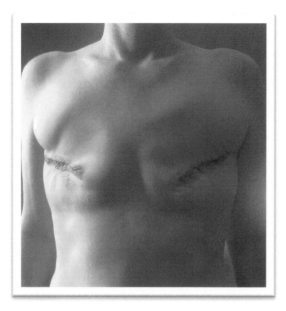

December 21ˢᵗ, two weeks after surgery. Dr. Rayhrer was able to leave enough breast tissue in the middle and on the bottom of both breasts to use as a base for the reconstruction.

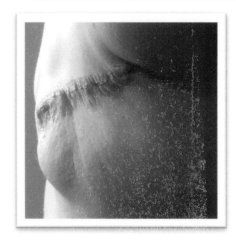

Both the left and right mastectomy incisions were covered with a thick, purple, medical glue that would stay on for several weeks during healing.

After she had cut the stitches that held the tubing in place, she yanked on the tube and almost a foot of tubing came out. I was focused on Wiley and watched his mouth fall open. He had a look of total shock and surprise on his face. I wasn't sure what was happening as I was looking at him, I think he mouthed "Oh, My Gosh," just as she gave the other side a big yank and that tube came out. Definitely not for the faint of heart.

The pain was intense the first few days after the mastectomy and I had to use opioid pain medication to be able to handle it. The pain meds caused severe constipation and I felt lethargic, itchy, and awful. On the fifth day after my double mastectomy, I stopped the prescription pain medicine and switched to CBD rich cannabis. I found that cannabis products reduced my pain after surgery and had the added benefit of allowing me a good night sleep. I kept my arms down at my sides to minimize the pain, but by the second week I was able to slowly raise my arms above my head, careful not to push them too far.

Before the surgery, I had a blood test to find out if I had the BRCA 1 or BRCA 2 breast cancer gene. There was a 50/50 chance that I had the genes. A positive BRCA gene increased my risk for reoccurrence and could also increase my odds of future cancers. Two weeks after my mastectomy, I received the news that I was negative for both BRCA genes. It was a great Christmas gift.

My entire family came to our home in Ojai for Christmas, just two weeks after my surgery. I had a hard time standing for very long and felt dizzy and exhausted. Everyone pitched in and we had a potluck style Christmas meal and I lounged on the chaise enjoying everyone's company. Afterwards, I found comfort as I soaked in a hot bath while I kept both incisions above the water. During the holidays friends came by for short visits and I slept a lot. My chest was traumatized and I had slowed way down to allow myself to heal.

Healing
December 31, 2015

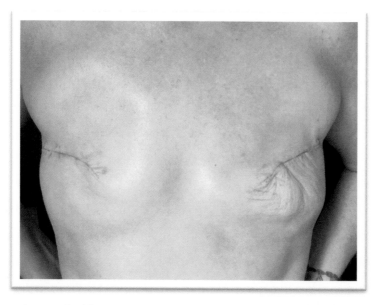

About three weeks post double mastectomy. All the glue was gone and the incisions were healing.
Left and right breast scars shown below.

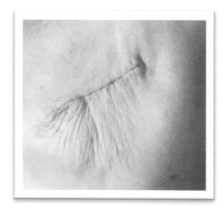

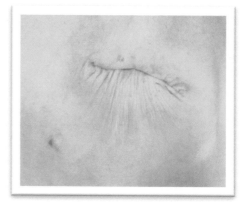

We spent New Year's Eve at home because I felt too tired to celebrate. It was a little over three weeks post-surgery and I was still sore and I struggled to extend my arms over my head. I spent two hours in the bath and gently removed the purple glue from both breasts with a wash cloth and soap. It never peeled off on its own and for some reason it still clung to my skin which made it uncomfortable when I moved. My incisions healed well, but it was tough to look in the mirror.

I hadn't realized how much my breasts had contributed to my sense of femininity and identity as a woman. My clothing no longer hung over my breasts but laid flat and uneven on my chest. I felt like a boy. When I felt ugly and unworthy, my inner voice stepped up and confirmed that I was still beautiful, still sexy but most importantly still alive. I didn't totally believe it.

I would cry most mornings at the sight of my scars. I hid my tears in the shower or while I laid in bed and pretended I was still asleep. I struggled with my new reality but didn't want everyone to know. I kept some of the sorrow and grief to myself. I had let a doctor cut my breasts off and I missed them and who I was before. After allowing myself a bit of pity, I would find that piece of me that was grateful and strong and move on with my day.

I had my first consultation with my cancer oncologist, Dr. Shilpa Shah. *The tumor was gone, but had any cancer cells escaped?* Even though the cancer had not spread to my lymph nodes, there was a chance that some cancer cells migrated via my lymphatic system during the surgery and hid somewhere in my body ready to rebound and multiply. Due to the fact that my cancer cells were considered very aggressive, Dr. Shah told me that chemotherapy was almost certain. However, the results of further testing would confirm my treatment options. The tumor removed from my left breast was sent to a lab in Northern California for an Oncotype DX test. The test would provide a prediction of chemotherapy benefit and give us more information to make treatment decisions. Not everyone benefits from the test, but in my case, the results showed that I would benefit from the addition of chemotherapy.

So many questions I needed answers to, but we had to wait and wait and wait for the test results. We had a teenager and we told him everything but we kept things as light as possible. We joked that my breast had gone to the bay area without me. *How did it get there? Was it in a plastic bag in the mail? What did they do with my breast tissue when they were done with it? Was it sitting in some freezer to be used for experiments? Was there a freezer filled with nipples in the Bay area?* It was funny the weird thoughts I had when I had nothing else to focus on. I kind of wanted to know but never pursued the answers because I thought it was a little warped.

I'm Still Me
January 7, 2016

We closed Kingston's Candy Co. on January 10th, 2016. My identity as the candy lady had ended. It was bittersweet. The week after we closed the candy store, Wiley and I headed to UCLA for a consultation with a genetic counselor. We wanted answers about my genes and their contribution to my breast cancer. The appointment with the specialist was covered by insurance so I took advantage of it. After going over our family history and looking at my cancer specifics with the genetic counselor we found out that there weren't many answers. None of the dozens of extra tests were covered by insurance and it meant thousands of dollars more spent out of pocket for tests that would result in more questions than answers. I hadn't received a bill from the double mastectomy yet, so we decided not to pursue any other genetic tests at that time.

While we waited for my chest to heal I met with my plastic surgeon, Dr. Samuel Bern, to discuss my breast reconstruction options and timeline. I had the option of choosing a trans flap breast reconstruction procedure that would use my own muscle and fat to create breasts without implants. It had its benefits but would be a twelve-hour surgery with months of recovery. I couldn't do another surgery of that magnitude and I told Dr. Bern that I was interested in the more standard breast reconstruction that used breast implants. We agreed to meet again, once I had recovered from my chemotherapy treatments.

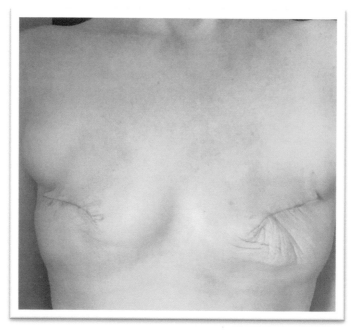

A little bit of cleavage left after surgery to aid in reconstruction later.

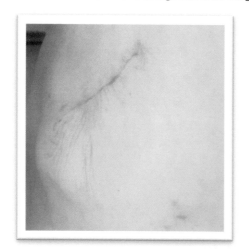 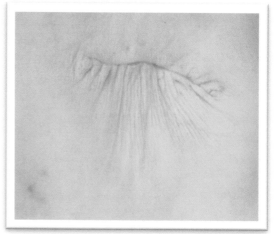

Left and right breasts - Small scars below each incision were from surgery drains.

I met my lymphatic therapist, Alicia Morris, every week to help with healing and to also prevent lymphedema in my arms. Due to the removal of four lymph nodes and all of my breast tissue, my lymphatic system was no longer able to move out lymph and toxins on its own. Lymphedema would occur if the lymph backed-up and created swelling in my arms. I was warned that once lymphedema took hold, it was very hard to reverse and would plague me for life. Even though I thought it was really worth-while, I had stopped weekly lymphatic appointments to save money and only went when I needed it. Each treatment had to be paid out of pocket because it was not covered by my medical insurance.

The cost of my breast cancer physically and mentally was huge. Financially it took a big toll on our savings, even though we had good medical insurance provided by Wiley's employer. It did not cover any alternative treatments, copays, or incidentals that you need to compliment the traditional treatments. The little things add up quickly; stool softeners, boxes of Benadryl®, daily probiotics, masks, gloves, prescription medicine copays, fragrance free beauty products, lymphatic treatments, and the list goes on and on. I felt fortunate that we had an emergency fund to draw from after I closed both businesses and lost my income. It wasn't easy watching our savings account slowly decline. Wiley was quick to remind me that cancer was an emergency and that it was exactly what our savings was for.

Chemotherapy was scheduled to start the first week of February. Wiley and I planned a weekend away in Napa at the end of January. Our 22nd wedding anniversary was going to be difficult that year because it was three days after chemo started. Napa gave us a break and a little time to ourselves. We pretended that everything was fine, but it wasn't. I feared chemo and the horror stories I had heard didn't help. I was surprised to find that some people chose to send me articles that condemned my choice of treatment and stated that chemotherapy was going to kill me. *Wow. Those people are horrible.* I ignored them and I became more confident in my choice. I took my treatment very seriously and had done a lot of research before I committed to it. I was not going to be scared out of treatment. I had a very aggressive cancer and refused to pretend otherwise. My parents treated illness as error and it killed them. I wanted to live.

Cancer Support
January 25, 2016

When I found out I had breast cancer, I was pleased to find out that there was a lot of cancer support in our little town. Susan Kapadia opened Ojai Cares, a cancer resource center in 2014 after she survived breast cancer. The center provided me with one on one support, group sessions, oncology massage, reiki healing, and overwhelming love and warmth. All free of charge. Ojai Cares' executive director, Renee Mandala, put me in touch with Kathy Hartley, owner of The Lavender Inn. Kathy had started a cancer retreat in 2009 called *INNcourage* which she held at the Inn. I was invited to attend the retreat where we were provided a safe environment to lounge in our pajamas for three days and two nights and share with other woman who had cancer. We each had a cozy room at the charming Inn and Kathy's staff provided all of our meals. We had a cooking class, a day of pampering that included a facial and massage, we took a hike up Shelf Road, and learned how to apply make-up sponsored by the American Cancer Society. We shared our personal experiences with cancer and got to know each other in between activities.

I was seven weeks post double mastectomy and felt self-conscious about how I looked. Nicole Jones, a vibrant, young, mother of two teenagers introduced herself and shared that she was a couple weeks away from a double mastectomy. Once she realized that I was newly recovered from a double, she asked if I would show her my scars. To that point, I had only shown my mother-in-law, two sisters, and a couple close friends, so I wasn't sure about showing someone I had just met. Nicole told me that she was very scared about her pending surgery and that was all I needed to hear to agree.

My other new friend, Martina Albert, wanted to know what they looked like too. We walked into the pantry off the Lavender Inn kitchen for a little privacy and I removed my shirt. Nicole's hands immediately went to cover her mouth. I took that as a bad sign, but Nicole let out a sigh of relief and said, "That's not so bad." *It isn't?* Both she and Martina were so positive and supportive toward the two enormous scars blazing across my chest. Nicole said, "I can totally do this." It was the moment when I realized that I didn't actually look like Frankenstein and that I could share what had happened to me to help other women. The idea for my book was born right then and there and the title *We Will Rebuild* seemed perfect. *Thank you, Nicole.*

Life coach, Brock Montagna, was on hand at the retreat and gave us each one-on-one support. I had never spoken with a life coach before and she immediately helped me identify the source of my conflict. My childhood religious indoctrination was still influencing my decision making and significantly contributing to my fear. One hour with Brock and my whole perspective transformed. I talked to other women that were in the middle of their chemo treatments and saw that it was not impossible to go through. It amazed me how close I got with eight other women in such a short time and I remain close to many of the women at the retreat.

Chapter Three: Practical Suggestions

- Interview your surgeon to make sure you both agree with the treatment recommendations.
- Take advantage of any available medical testing to gain insights about your cancer and treatment options.
- Inquire about the details of your upcoming surgery and your recovery process.
- If your state allows, have your surgeon prescribe all meds before surgery, so you have them on hand.
- If you choose to use cannabis, find out the laws in your state and visit a dispensary for help choosing products. If possible purchase before surgery so you have it when you need it.
- Stock up on prune juice and stool softeners or laxatives as the pain meds can cause severe constipation depending on the length of time you use it.
- Plan to have a close friend or family member help you for at least the first week, more if they are available.
- Schedule as much time off from work and life as possible. You will need lots of time to heal.
- Find a cancer support center in your area and take advantage of their services and support.
- Talk to friends and family that have gone through breast cancer to get perspective and advice.
- You may receive unsolicited advice and it's ok to ignore it if you don't agree.
- You can thank people for their concern, but don't be afraid to shut down anyone that oversteps their boundaries. It is stressful enough without having to hear doom and gloom scenarios that don't affect you.
- Take another deep breath, this journey is long, you are stronger than you think.

Chapter Four
The Dreaded Chemotherapy
February 2, 2016

Dr. Shah wanted me to recover and heal as much as possible from the double mastectomy before we started four rounds of chemo. We waited two full months before beginning treatment and the chemo rounds would be spaced three weeks apart to allow my body time to recover. I was grateful for the time to heal from my double mastectomy but still nervous about everything I had heard about chemotherapy.

There are **four stages of cancer** that determine how far the cancer has spread:[i]
- Stage 0 means the cancer cells are right where they started and have not spread.
- Stage 1 cancers are localized to one part of the body.
- Stage 2 cancers are growing but have only extended to the nearby lymph nodes.
- Stage 3 cancers are considered advanced and have spread beyond the lymph nodes, possibly to the muscle, but not too distant organs.
- Stage 4 cancers are the most advanced stage and the progression is known as metastasis. The cancer has spread to multiple parts of the body including organs.

There are also **three levels of grading** that describe what the tumor cancer cells look like and how fast they are growing (aggressiveness):[ii]
- Grade 1 are small and uniform in size and the slowest growing cancer cells.
- Grade 2 are slightly bigger than normal cells and growing faster than normal.
- Grade 3 cancer cells look different than normal cells and are the fastest growing.

There are different classifications for non-invasive breast cancers. Instead of 1, 2, and 3, they are graded as low, medium, or high.

My breast cancer was invasive because it had broken out of the duct. My aggressiveness was considered grade three, the most aggressive. When my cancer cells were looked at under a microscope they were whooping it up and I was told they looked like they were having a party. A fun way to describe very real risks.

I had always been a go-getter. My sisters and I got that from our dad. Our informal family motto was "We get shit done." If chemo would reduce my overall long-term risk by a huge margin statistically, I knew I had to stick with my motto. It was hard laying around the house recovering from the loss of my breasts and I was about to do it again during chemo. I was gearing up to poison my body with the hopes that any stray cancer cells would be killed and I could resume my life as if nothing had happened. I knew that was never going to be the case. The reality was hard to grasp. Chemo could damage my organs, my hair, my skin, and my life. *Was chemo-brain a real thing? Was I going to end up with it? Who was I going to be at the end of chemo?*

I could just say NO, and not do chemo, but I realized I needed to do it for Wiley, Vance, and the rest of my family and friends. I followed my intuition and scheduled the appointment for my first chemo treatment. Wiley would drive me and be there for support.

A close friend's mom, Sherry, also a breast cancer survivor, told me about an anti-nausea patch called Sancuso® that her friend had used during her treatment. I asked my oncologist about it and she agreed to order it for me. I was told without insurance it was very expensive, hundreds of dollars for one patch, but with my insurance, it would be around $75. I figured it was worth the money if it prevented nausea. I was grateful to be in contact with other breast cancer survivors that could share their knowledge.

Round One

February 2, 2016

The evening before chemo I took a steroid pill and placed the Sancuso® anti-nausea patch on my arm. I didn't notice any side effects from either medication, that was a good start. The day of chemo, I came fully prepared. I brought a cooler with string cheese, crackers, nuts, protein bars, ginger candy for nausea, a large bottle of organic grape sports drink, and a 96-oz. cup of ice chips from 7-eleven. Another friend told me that it could cause horrible mouth sores, but sucking on ice chips during the infusions could prevent the painful sores from developing. It worked, I never got any mouth sores.

I also lugged along a tote bag that contained an eye mask if I wanted to nap, my iPad to go online, adult coloring books and felt pens to be creative, a juicy romance novel to escape, my journal to document, anti-nausea pills, hand moisturizer, lip balm, tissues and much more. It was so heavy, Wiley had to carry it. I looked like I was moving in. In hindsight, it was ridiculous the amount of stuff I lugged to my first round, but I wanted to be prepared for anything.

I chose the big, brown, leather reclining chair next to the window at the end of the room, it had the best view; the parking lot. I was one of five other men and women undergoing some form of treatment that day. They all seemed comfortable and the mood in the room was light, so my initial fear disappeared.

The nurses, Kayla and Shristi, brought me a warm blanket, a heating pad to warm up my arms before the IV was inserted, and a pillow to rest my arms on during treatment. My legs were reclined and I settled in. The nurses were awesome.

Since it was my first treatment, Kayla told me what she would be doing every step of the way. Each infusion was done separately along with IV fluids to help prevent dehydration. First came a dose of anti-nausea medication even though I was already wearing a patch for that very purpose. After about half an hour I received a dose of steroids to reduce inflammation, and later I was administered Benadryl®, an antihistamine to prevent possible allergic reactions. The Benadryl® immediately made my eyes droop and my remaining nervousness disappeared. I was so drowsy that I ended up watching multiple episodes of a popular home makeover show that was on HGTV®. I never even brought out any of the items I had dragged along for entertainment.

After a couple hours in the chair, I was ready for the "big guns." My oncologist had instructed the nurses to take things slowly until we knew I could tolerate each of the drugs. The last thing we wanted to deal with was an adverse reaction. I had always been very sensitive to prescription medications. The first chemo drug, Cyclophosphamide®, yes, it sounded scary to me too, took about an hour and a half for it to drip into my vein and was administered at half the dose. That was about twice as long as normal, so if I had a reaction, they would immediately stop the infusion. We moved onto the second chemo drug, Taxotere®, which took another hour and a half. I was in the chair for six hours that first day and exhausted. A combination of the drugs and all of the worrying had tapped my energy and strength.

Groggy, but feeling pretty good.

I was prepared to be vomiting and nauseated during and after chemo but was surprised at how well I felt. I was convinced that it was the combo of steroids and Benadryl®. That night I took another steroid pill before bed and took anti-nausea pills every six hours, just in case.

The day after my first round, I woke up with a hot, flushed face, I was tired but felt pretty good. I got out of bed, was able to eat some biscuits and binge watched *Downton Abbey*. The second day, I felt tired but not as flushed. I had continued the anti-nausea pills and kept the Sancuso® patch on for three full days as directed.

Nobody warned me that the amount of anti-nausea medication I consumed would shut down my digestive system. I suffered for three days before the constipation was resolved with a combination of organic prunes, organic prune juice, stool softeners, and Metamucil. I learned this lesson the hard way, yes, the HARD way. I did not want my constipation adventure repeated, so I ditched the anti-nausea pills for the next round and used just the patch.

Every single Friday after chemo treatment started, I had to go to the local blood lab for a complete blood count (CBC). My oncologist monitored my blood cell counts to make sure the levels did not drop too low. Low blood counts could cause all kinds of symptoms and could be dangerous because my body would not be able to fight off infection. The chemo was a badass destroyer and my blood counts had probably dropped substantially after only three days. My blood test results would not be back until the following week. I felt exhausted, dizzy, short of breath, and unable to walk across the room.

The chemo drugs targeted all of the dividing cells in my body, good and bad cells and prevented them from multiplying. Cancer cells divide quickly, so chemo prevented that from happening. Unfortunately, it cannot differentiate between the cancer cells and the normal cells and they would all be destroyed. One of the side effects of chemotherapy was the loss of healthy white blood cells which left my body without a functioning immune system.

If my blood count was unable to rise on its own, a shot of blood cell growth factor would be needed to force them back up. Blood cell growth factors are substances produced by the body that stimulate the cells in the bone marrow to produce more red blood cells, white blood cells, or platelets.[iii] My oncologist was concerned about my symptoms and had me return to her office that Friday where they gave me a Neupogen® shot in the stomach. I was told it was very painful in the arm, but if they folded my stomach fat over and placed the needle into that, there would only be a little sting and no pain. Since my levels were probably low, the nurse would give us another dose of the shot for Sunday which would be administered by Wiley if needed. The nurse gave him a brief lesson and sent us home.

I had never heard anyone talk about the pain that was involved with chemo, but I woke up that first morning after the shot and was pretty sure that I might die from the bone pain. It was random and intermittent pain that would attack a bone or joint in my body, reduce me to tears and then move onto another bone or joint. Agony was the best word to describe my pain. I didn't want to use any opioids instead I continued to use CBD rich cannabis products to help me cope with the pain.

After the second shot on Sunday, my body reacted by covering me in red, itchy hives from head to toe. In addition, my vision was blurred, it hurt to open my eyes, and I had a painful headache. I phoned the on-call, weekend oncologist, and was told that I was having an adverse reaction to Neupogen®. I was instructed to take a daily steroid pill and a dose of Benadryl® every four to six hours for the hives. I was in a drugged-up fog and miserable. The results from my first blood test came back and my blood count was dangerously low after the first round as my oncologist had suspected. I was lethargic and unable to climb out of bed until the following Thursday.

At my first round of chemo, an IV pumped five different pharmaceuticals into my body, not to mention the steroid pill, the anti-nausea patch, and some antibiotics. Looking back, it was a miracle the eight different drugs they gave me that day hadn't caused an adverse reaction, but one little shot in the stomach did. I had never experienced medical intervention on that level when I was growing up in a Christian Science home. *CANCER SUCKS!*

At my two-week follow up appointment with my oncologist, I told her that I would rather be dead than have another Neupogen® shot. She told me that was an option. Ha! She explained that without the shot, my blood cell count would remain dangerously low and I could either die or wind up in the hospital from a common flu or cold. I was advised to limit visitors to the house if they had been in contact with anyone that was sick in the last 72 hours. I texted every visitor beforehand and told them they had to be flexible and check in with me the morning of their visit. I would feel ok one minute and then down the next. My friends and family were all very accommodating.

During the first round of chemo I started to experience hot flashes, the kind of heat that slowly rose from the neck up and then engulfed my whole body in what felt like internal flames. As the weeks went on, the hot flashes became more frequent, lasted longer, and produced a lot of sweat. I slept on a beach towel which kept my side of the bed dry. Some nights I got out of bed and exchanged the soaked towel for a dry one. It was hellacious. Another possible side effect they told me about was the end of my menstrual cycle. I was on my period the week of my very first round and it would be the last cycle I had for over 400 days after chemo ended. In women under age 40, the chances of menopause being temporary are greater than women over 40. Chemotherapy could permanently damage my ovaries and I could be forced into early menopause.

I slept quite a bit those first couple weeks and allowed my body to dictate what I could and couldn't do. I knew that if my blood levels did not rise, I would not be able to continue treatment every three weeks. Changing my chemo schedule could diminish the effectiveness of the treatment and might not kill potential cancer cells. I was not going to fail at the ultimate goal and I agreed that I would do the stomach shot, but only if it was absolutely necessary. The next week's CBC showed that the two shots had indeed done what they were supposed to do. My blood count was up enough that I was cleared for my next round, a short three weeks after the first one.

Three weeks might seem like a long time to recover from treatment, but it wasn't. Nothing had prepared me for the agonizing symptoms that came with chemotherapy. Just as I felt a bit better it was time to gear up for another round. I dreaded round two but realized I would be half way done with the treatment. I wasn't known for giving up once I had started something and I wanted this whole shit show to be over, so I pressed forward.

A friend and fellow survivor told me that she bulked up on red meat just after her chemo treatments and was able to discontinue the evil stomach shots. I was willing to try just about anything to avoid the symptoms that came with the shot. For me, the effects of the chemo were not as bad as the effects of the shot. Wiley went out to the local meat market and picked out some organic, grass fed steaks and they were amazing. I think my body was just glad it had some iron to help it recover. Even though I had not experienced any nausea with the first round, I felt horrible and all I wanted to eat was comfort food.

Certain foods no longer smelled or tasted like they used to, but some foods retained their charm, so those were the foods I stuck with. Breakfast was eggs fried in grass fed Irish butter, sour dough toast slathered in butter, and no nitrate bacon cooked just past pink and before it was crispy. Lunch was biscuits and mashed potatoes or a simple bean and cheese burrito, nothing fancy. Red meat, mashed potatoes and green vegetables sounded the best for dinner. No alcohol, no sugar, no preservatives, no pesticides or chemically processed foods were advised during chemo and they didn't even sound good anyway. My oncologist confirmed it was best to eat what sounded good and not to worry too much about anything else. If I kept it down that was a win-win. That diet was sure to ruin my figure, but surviving was the goal, so I ate what sounded and tasted the best.

Going through chemotherapy with a teenage boy in the house was going to be fun. NOT. Vance became quite critical of everything that I said or did and thought it was fine to comment without any filter on my appearance. I not only felt like shit but I was not going to win any awards for beauty. My skin became pale, I had dark circles under my eyes, and I was prone to crying at the drop of a hat. Teenage boys hate that shit. After one particular round of ridicule from Vance, I unbuttoned the top of my shirt and exposed the five-inch thick scar that was where my breast and nipple used to reside. "See this, I have another one just like it on the other side," I said to Vance. "This is not only physically painful but mentally. I have a hard time looking at myself in the mirror every morning and you are not helping. Do you want to see the other side?" Vance stared at me with a mix of horror and surprise.

I had never intended on showing my 15-year-old son the scars but holy shit! I was fighting for my life and he was worried about how I looked and he was being really mean to me. I realized that Vance was just as scared as I was, but he had decided that putting up a brick wall and treating me like he didn't care was the easiest way for him to deal. Luckily, that visual jolted Vance out of his ill-conceived plan and he began to talk openly about my cancer and what it meant for all of us. If he started to revert to being mean and pushing me away, all I had to say was, "Vance, do you need to see my scars again?" His response was always, "NO, I get it, I don't need to see them again." I even received an apology from him for his behavior. Sheesh.

There was so much down time during cancer treatment. There were often days, weeks, and months between doctor's appointments and sometimes it felt like I was fending for myself. I had to invent new ways to cope and complete the never-ending days. Thank goodness for creative care packages that came in the mail from some of my oldest and dearest friends. My friend Stephine had kept up with my life on social media and sent me the best gift. She sent me a *Dammit! Doll®* which was a faceless, cloth doll that was sewn together in the shape of a person. It had blue hair and was in a cool Indian paisley pattern. On the front of the doll there was a cute saying: "Whenever things don't go so well, and you want to hit the wall and yell, here's a little Dammit Doll, that you can't do without. Just grasp it firmly by the legs and find a place to slam it, and as you whack the stuffing out, yell Dammit! Dammit! Dammit!"® [iv]

We got a good laugh out of that doll, not to mention quite a few whacks followed by some swearing a little bit more vulgar than dammit. You can purchase a Dammit Doll online and I would highly recommend it as a humorous gift. I also received a Zen Buddhist calendar from my friend Jamie that I used to track the days when treatment would be over. It had soothing Asian inspired photos and ancient, peaceful quotes to relax the mind and bring out my inner peace.

Adult coloring books arrived too. With all of the down time during chemo and the self-imposed quarantine, I had to keep myself occupied. I bought a set of nice felt pens and took to coloring in elaborate drawings that contained either swear words or if I felt mellow, Buddhist mandalas and statues. When I finished a drawing, I wrote a note on it and gave it to one of my visitors. It took 30 years and a major illness to reintroduce me to coloring books and I was glad to be back. After three weeks of coping, it was time to gear up for round two. Round two would bring me half way through my treatments and closer to breast reconstruction and my new life. I think I can, I think I can, I think I can.

Who Needs Hair Anyway?
February 15, 2016

Even though I had been warned, I hadn't prepared for the shock of my hair falling out as a result of chemo. It was the day after Valentine's Day and it hadn't even been two weeks since my first chemo treatment. I thought I had more time. I stared at my reflection in the bathroom mirror and wondered when it was going to fall out. I gently grabbed a clump of my hair in each fist. I fully expected it to hold onto my scalp for dear life and resist my tugging. It didn't. It just came right out in both hands as I gasped and yelled for Wiley. He stared at the clumps of strawberry blond hair I held in my hands and without flinching announced it was time to shave my head.

You would think Wiley would be mortified by the idea of a bald wife, but the inner punk rocker that had laid dormant for several decades had come back to life. When I thought ahead to that moment, I expected Vance, my less than empathetic teenage son, to be in on the shaving. It seemed like the perfect time for him to release all of his anger and frustration on my hair. Unfortunately, or maybe fortunately, Vance was quarantined to his bedroom with a nasty cold. He wasn't allowed within a few feet of me and I had to protect myself with a hospital mask and obsessive hand washing anytime he left his confines.

Instead, I had a giddy, smiling husband that was way too excited about his new task. We exchanged smiles and giggles and Wiley started in with the electric shaver. I felt like a dog being shaved for Summer as he ran it against my scalp using the closest attachment he owned. Back in our teenage years and early twenties, we thought of ourselves as rebels. We dressed in black and had crazy hairstyles dyed in Manic Panic® colors. Some of my closest friends had brightly colored Mohawks, it was the 1980's and totally appropriate. However, it was now 2016 and I was 46 years old, married with a teenage son, and considered middle aged. Hardly the time to sport a Mohawk, but under the circumstances, the perfect time for anarchy.

Wiley lovingly shaped my hair into a Mohawk and stood it up with product. The crazy, fun-loving anarchist wife was back, but not for long. I wore the Mohawk for about 30 minutes and then decided it wasn't for me. It was time to finish the job and cut the remainder of my hair off. Wiley made quick work of it and before I knew it, my beloved golden locks were spread all over the bathroom floor. It wasn't as bad as I thought it was going to be, because Wiley made it fun. There was just a small bit of hair that still clung to my scalp. It was short enough that it could fall out without any further trauma to my ego.

Who knew shaving my head could be so much fun.

Round Two
February 23, 2016

Rockin' my new bald look.

A week after we shaved my head, I went in for round two of chemo. I felt more prepared for that round as I had survived the first. I had gained some valuable lessons about coping with the symptoms and Wiley managed to keep me on track. I had been warned by other survivors that the chemo treatments were cumulative as they progressed. I wasn't really sure what that meant. I continued to smile my way through it and tried to make the best of a bad situation.

Exactly three weeks after the first lesson in chemo, I was back in my padded recliner chair next to the window in the chemo room at my oncologist's office. I was grateful that the universe decided that I had dibs on that chair and it was available all four rounds. It provided me with a shred of stability in that unstable landscape.

Since I tolerated the half dose of the Cyclophosphamide® last time, my oncologist was boosting it 15% to a 65% dosage. We were still worried about the effects of the drug on my body and the ability to metabolize it. All of the other drugs went in at full strength and full speed. I only spent four hours in the chair that day and it was good to be finishing the treatment much faster. I hadn't dragged an entire suitcase full of items with me that time. I just brought a few snacks in a cooler, along with my ice chips, and plenty of liquids to drink. I spent my woozy Benadryl® infused morning watching the HGTV® and occasionally chit chatting with the nurses and other patients. It was a pleasant experience lacking the anxiety of the unknown from the first round.

I was elated to be half way done even though the next three weeks post chemo brought all the horror and discomfort of the first, but I managed it better. The constipation was held at bay by drinking 90 ounces of liquids each day. That 90 ounces included, 16 ounces of full strength coffee in the morning, two glasses of Metamucil mixed with prune juice, one in the morning and one in the evening, lots and lots of water, and a stool softener when needed. I had discontinued my anti-nausea pills and kept the nausea away with the Sancuso® patch and cannabis. I waited for the blood test results to determine if the Neupogen® shot would be absolutely necessary. That bought me an extra week without it.

The blood test came back showing my numbers had dropped even further. My oncologist had sent me home with a couple vials of the evil stuff and we kept it in the butter tray on the refrigerator door. It had to be kept cold until use. Wiley shot me up a week after the chemo was administered and the terrible symptoms including bone pain, unrelenting night sweats, body aches, hives, and a sense of death in all of my cells settled in.

The following week's blood test proved that only one shot was needed to bring my numbers back up to an acceptable level and that was definitely better than two. I was eating quite a bit of red meat in hopes that it would boost my blood levels. Meat and potatoes were my favorite thing for dinner, but I wasn't used to that much red meat, so Wiley added other basic comfort foods, like his great-grandma's baked macaroni and cheese and simple pastas. With the increased calories in my diet and the major decrease in activity, I started to put on weight, but I didn't care. Most of my days were spent in my pajamas at home and an extra ten pounds was of no real concern. Comfort food made me feel better and I figured I had plenty of time to lose the weight after treatment ended.

Round Three
March 15, 2016

Round three. It sounded like I was in a boxing match and most days it felt like it. By that time, all of my hair had fallen out leaving me with a smooth head. When the hair follicles died off around my second round of chemo, I had the strangest sensation in my scalp. It was as if every single hair follicle was screaming in pain begging me to stop the treatments. It felt like someone yanked a hair out and then it would ache. It was strange and uncomfortable, especially when I was prone to hot flashes that covered my scalp and the rest of my body in an instant flash of moisture. When they say your hair falls out, they mean ALL your hair. Every single hair on my body was killed off and sent down the drain in the shower. I was smooth as silk and missing my eye lashes and eyebrows. The only upside to being hairless was I no longer had to shave.

Round three was finally here and I settled into my usual recliner near the window and Kayla hooked me up to my IV. A few minutes into my treatment, a woman came in and sat down next to me. I recognized her from the last chemo treatment. She started to talk to me and in between sentences she was coughing a lot. I asked her what was wrong and she said that she was sick with a cold and had a fever that she had caught from a family member. She explained that it was her last chemo treatment and she refused to miss it.

I avoided illness during my chemo treatments up to this point and was dismayed that a sick woman sat right down next to me without any care or concern for my well-being. I asked her if she would please move to another chair and I called the nurse over. I told Kayla that I only had one more chemo after that one and that if I got sick it could jeopardize my remaining treatments. I questioned why someone with a fever was allowed to put the rest of us in harm's way. They moved her to another chair and put a mask on her. They were very sympathetic to her because it was her last chemo treatment and she wanted them to end. I understood. Really, I did, but it did not sit well with me that they were breaking their own rules and that put us all at risk. I was told that her fever was low and I had nothing to worry about. I was worried. I had been told to worry about illness by my oncologist in that very office. *Why was her last chemo more important than everyone else's health?*

I had kept quiet in the past when confronted with things that challenged me, but breast cancer had taught me to be my own advocate and to stand up for myself. I got up a few times and rolled my IV bags with me to the bathroom to wash my hands. I took a breather to release my anxiety. I was paranoid and I had every right to be. I tried to make the best of the situation. I thought about the actors on TV and in the movies, that walked around the hospital with an IV bag hooked to a metal rolling stand. Every three weeks I awkwardly moved between the chemo chair and the bathroom. My main objective was to not tip the stand over or run it into anything. When I went to the bathroom, I carefully moved the tubing around, so it wouldn't attach to the door knob or sink handle. I would loop it around my arm to keep from dipping it in the toilet or peeing on it. No wonder it looked so easy to negotiate in the movies, they didn't actually have an IV in their arm and they weren't really worried about it being ripped out. With the amount of liquids being put in my IV and the giant 96 oz. cup of ice chips I sucked on, I got up every hour. Comfortable clothes I could pull up and down with one hand were essential. If I moved my arm too much it would hurt with the IV needle clinging to my vain.

The chemo room was chilly, but the relentless hot flashes required me to quickly rip back my layers of clothing to find relief. Once covered in a thin layer of sweat, the chill of the room caught up to me and I slowly put back on my layers. It was a never-ending dance of heat and chill.

After resigning myself to being in the same very small room with a woman that was sick with a cold, I had to let it go. Shortly after, her husband arrived with a cake for all of us to share. It was her eighth and final chemo treatment and she had completed it. I never thought about celebrating in the chemo room but loved the idea. I shared a piece of the ultra-sweet cake and pushed all of the frosting off to the side because my taste buds couldn't handle it. That celebration and that slice of cake pushed my fear aside and I forgave her for her selfishness. I realized I was really happy for her and I might do the same thing if I were in her shoes.

Chemo was grueling and the three weeks in between never felt like enough. I spent my days either in bed or on our chaise in the living room entertaining myself with adult coloring books or reading. I tried to watch movies, but I didn't seem to be able to tolerate much violence on the big screen. It was all too much of a reminder of the suffering and violence I felt I was going through with cancer. I already felt like I had one foot in the grave and anything might nudge me off into the abyss. I was also emotional and prone to crying, so tear jerkers weren't an option either.

That third round of chemo was done at 100% of the dose since I had tolerated the reduced doses in round one and two. I was covered in hives and my eyes and face were very swollen. I looked like humpty dumpty ready to fall off the wall and crack my smooth shell open. I continued taking a daily combo of steroids and Benadryl® to relieve the symptoms as instructed by my oncologist. I didn't even look like myself anymore. That excessive number of steroids was apparently too much for me. I woke up one morning with a very swollen face and I no longer wanted to live. I had never experienced depression or desperation in my life, and it caught me off guard. I spent that whole day wishing that there was a bridge outside my home that I could step off of and end my nightmare. I contemplated taking my own life.

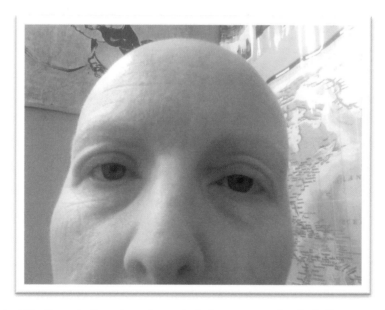

I looked like Humpty-Dumpty and my whole face was swollen including my eyelids.

Luckily, the recognition of that major mood change was not lost on me and I phoned my oncologist to talk about it. She explained that the effects of the steroids were cumulative and she recommended I discontinue them completely and fight the hives and swelling with Benadryl® alone. I was glad my oncologist instantly knew that the problem was the steroids. It was scary to have side effects that threatened my very existence. I immediately stopped the steroids and it felt like I had a handle on the other symptoms since I knew exactly what to expect;

- The day of chemo, I always felt groggy but good.
- The day after, I was tired, flushed and hot, but still felt good.
- The third day, I was down, in bed, unable to read or watch TV. Intermittent crying or laughing at Wiley's jokes relieved my misery.
- The fourth and fifth day after chemo kept me usually in bed or laying on the chaise in the living room.
- I felt horrible and knew that in a few days, just when I was starting to feel a little better, I would need a Neupogen® shot.
- After the Neupogen® shot, I would be down for another three to five days experiencing agonizing bone and muscle pain and an overall feeling of sickness.
- After the shot wore off and my CBC showed my blood levels had been boosted, I was able to get up and move around the house.
- After three weeks, I felt like myself again and enjoyed my day without all of the horrible symptoms of the first two weeks.
- Then, I did it all over again.

Some days I would go for a ride with Wiley in the car to pick Vance up from ninth grade. I would work on a puzzle, read, binge watch BBC shows, color in my coloring books or spend hours on Facebook. It was incredibly boring, but visitors broke up the monotony and gave me hope that I still had a life out there waiting for me once I recovered.

It had been one month since I had my last menstrual cycle and the day came and went without another. I soon realized that the chemo had shut down my ovaries and my period. I felt the lack of hormones was affecting my mood, but there was a chance, a small chance, that my period would return after chemo ended. I was told that 85% of women my age would go into permanent menopause as a result of my type of chemo. I didn't care, I had a teenager and no desire to start all over again in that department. If it was gone, then I would just accept it and move on. One more loss for the home team, but maybe it really wasn't a loss after all. I would have to go through menopause fairly soon anyway since I was nearing 50, so I resigned myself to the idea of early menopause.

Bald with no eyelashes, very few eyebrows, but I still smiled when I could.

Round Four
April 5, 2016

My fourth and final chemo treatment seemed like it would never arrive, but it did. Two days before my 47th birthday I arrived at my oncologist's office ready to celebrate the ending of that stage of treatment. I was hairless, I had gained ten pounds, and I was covered in red blotchy hives. I felt so bad at times that I was sure that was what it felt like to be dying. My mastectomy scars had healed very well over the course of four months and I would soon be planning breast reconstruction. The aching and soreness from the surgery was gone. I was a little concerned about the redness of my scars, but nobody else seemed concerned.

That last chemo day was closure from all of the nastiness I had endured over the last two months. I never wanted to sit in that chair and stare out that window again. I arrived at my last chemo prepared to throw a party. We stopped at Trader Joes on the way to chemo and picked up lemon cupcakes with light pink frosting. I had spent the week that led up to that last chemo, decorating a poster board that celebrated all of my milestones. It was beginning to sink in that someday soon, I was going to be a cancer survivor. It was not only my last round of chemo, it was also my 47th birthday, the third anniversary of my heart drama, and I was almost done with all of it.

My forties were not turning out the way I thought they would, but I was still alive and kicking!

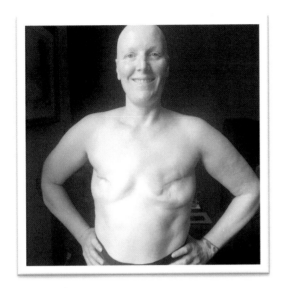

It was my 47th birthday and I wasn't going to let being bald and covered in red, itchy, hives ruin it. We celebrated my birthday and last chemo with light pink cupcakes. They looked like breasts to me.

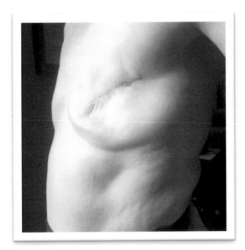
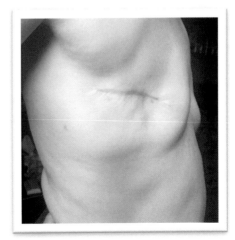

Left and right breast incisions were healing well and you could start to see where the breast implants would fit.

I went into that fourth round with a lot of positivity and thankfulness. I had endured the previous three rounds gaining in knowledge with each round. I knew what was coming and I could handle it. Piece of cake. Since it was my last round, my oncologist met with me right after my chemo treatment was done that same day to talk about the next steps. I knew that breast reconstruction was up next. She had also previously warned me that I was going to need to start Tamoxifen®, an anti-cancer drug very soon. That made me nervous because she wanted me on it for five to ten years and I knew that I would probably not be able to handle that.

Since I was still considered pre-menopausal, Tamoxifen® was the only drug option that I had. I was told that if at some point I was considered to be in menopause, there was another class of drugs called aromatase inhibitors that offered multiple choices and less side effects. It bothered me that I only had one choice because I had known many women that were still not in menopause that had breast cancer. Most women that I had spoken to had some side effects from it and the list of possible side effects gave me nightmares. My best chance of being fully recovered from the aggressive cancer resulted in everything I had already done plus Tamoxifen®. *Why was there only one drug offered for hormonal breast cancers for the last 40 years? Where were all the researchers and why hadn't they invented another option?*

With chemo completed, I had three whole months off from my oncologist. I really liked her, but was glad to get a break from the medical world. My next appointment was scheduled for July 5th, the day after Independence Day. I would go to the blood lab one week before my appointment to have a blood test that would measure my tumor markers for the first time. Tumor markers are substances found at higher than normal levels in the blood. Different types of cancers created different types of tumor markers depending on the disease process.[v] A blood test was the most common way to measure tumor markers. My type of breast cancer made a protein called CA 15-3. The tumor marker results would let us know if I still had cancer and at what level. I was also warned that the tumor marker test was not full proof and a good reading didn't necessarily mean that I was cancer free, but it was a good indication.

I was told that there was a healthy level for tumor markers and that I wanted to be within those limits. Higher numbers indicated active cancer and obviously that was not good. I knew deep down that my cancer was gone, but I needed confirmation to relax. I told Dr. Shah my fears and she told me to enjoy my time off, that we had done everything we could, and the results would be good. After she answered all of my questions and eased my fears, she sent me on my way to deal with the side effects of the final round of chemo.

My biggest complaint besides the chemo was the intense hot flashes that had started to occur after chemo started and my period ended. I relieved them the best I could with cold packs and iced drinks. Two days after round four, I managed to rally for my birthday and went out to a local restaurant with Wiley, Vance and a few friends for dinner. I no longer kept myself isolated from people and potential illness. I felt really good, but each day's symptoms seemed to be ten times worse than anything I had experienced to date. I frantically googled and found out that that the fourth round and any rounds after were considered the worst. Some of the long-term side effects to look out for from chemo include:[vi]

- Fatigue
- Difficulty focusing (chemo-brain)
- Early menopause
- Heart problems
- Reduced lung capacity
- Nerve damage or neuropathy resulting in numbness and tingling
- Muscle weakness and bone or joint issues
- Possibility of a secondary cancer

On more than one day, I found myself curled in a fetal position on my living room floor crying and wishing that I were dead. Holy shit. This round was way worse than I had anticipated and I started to wonder if I would survive it. To that point, I had been able to avoid all nausea, but it kicked in and my stomach constantly churned. Saliva accumulated in my mouth and I felt like I would vomit. The anti-nausea patch seemed like it had lost its effectiveness, but I was not going back to the anti-nausea pills and severe constipation. I found that a combination of sucking on CBD rich lozenges and wearing a CBD rich cannabis patch on my wrist kept the nausea under control. I never did throw up, but I ran to the bathroom on several occasions thinking it was inevitable. The days after round four seemed to be the longest of my life.

As a child, I was so scared of needles and had little to no experience with them, but I was no longer afraid. Twelve Fridays in a row I had shown up at the blood lab and they stuck me with a needle. After that many needle sticks, the spot where the needle went in had developed a small amount of scar tissue and bruised a little every week. *I wondered if people looked at my arm and thought I was a junkie? I doubt it, the bald head screamed cancer to everyone around me.* I looked exactly what you would imagine a cancer victim would look like. I often noticed people's compassionate looks or sometimes a little fear in their eyes. My cancer reminded people that life was impermanent, and people hated to be reminded of their own mortality.

I called my oncologist for the results of my weekly blood test and she told me that my results were dangerously low again. They were the lowest they had been and that was most likely why I felt so terrible. I needed one last Neupogen® shot, but I didn't want it. I tried to talk my way out of it, but my oncologist said I had to. "Why? I don't have any more chemo treatments" I pleaded with her, "I just want my blood levels to rise on their own, I don't need the shot." She explained that my levels would not rise rapidly, and my immune system could be severely depressed for months putting me in continuous danger of infection. Reluctantly, I went into the office that week for my fifth and final shot.

74

I had refused to bring one of the shots home with me on my last chemo round, even though they insisted. I was too optimistic and didn't want to believe that I was going to need another one. Oh well, I tried.

Wiley and Vance had bought me a 3-D puzzle of Paris for my birthday and I spent every single day laying on the living room floor building that puzzle. The first level of the puzzle was Paris back in the 15th century, the second level sat on top of that one and was the city we know today. The third level was all of the 3-D buildings and bridges winding along the Seine River.

It took me three weeks to complete it. Some days I would just lay next to it and stare at the pieces, too weak and sick to pick up the puzzle pieces and search for the place they fit. I was like that puzzle, I too had been broken into little pieces, scattered about, once whole and put together. I was a shell of my former self, but I was done. I could pick up those pieces, put them back in the box and put that away for good. Time to move on. I had a lot of healing to do and I needed to set my sights on breast reconstruction.

At that point, I was convinced that saline breast implants were the way to go. I had heard horror stories about silicone implants and how they could slowly leak into the body and make you sick. Saline seemed healthier and simpler. It was strange to be considering breast implants at all as I had never even contemplated that for myself, but I couldn't imagine myself without breasts. I felt like mine were missing. I understood why women would choose not to reconstruct. At the time, I spoke with several women that had decided against implants and were happy with their choice. I realized that there was no right or wrong answer, it was a matter of personal choice.

I phoned my plastic surgeon, Dr. Samuel Bern, the one I met back in January for a consultation. That appointment seemed like a lifetime ago. His office said they wanted me to be at least four weeks past my last chemo treatment before they would put in my breast tissue expanders. I decided to wait six weeks to allow myself more time to recover before surgery. I hadn't realized how much I missed my breasts until I scheduled to put in the expanders where my breasts used to be. That was the first step in reconstruction and I felt excited about it.

Margarita Time
April 24, 2016

Almost three weeks after chemo ended, a margarita sounded good. We celebrated at our very favorite Mexican restaurant, Los Caporales in Ojai. A bonus was all of the smiles and hugs from the Salinas family that owned the restaurant. Los Caporales was in the same building that the candy store used to be in and I smelled their handmade food and saw them almost every single day for six years. I was really happy to be there with them. Wiley ordered an extra shot of tequila to celebrate as he had been on duty most days as caretaker.

It had been three weeks since my last round of chemo and I had a hard time ignoring the little voice in my head. *What if my cancer wasn't gone? What if my tumor markers were too high? What if I did all of that treatment and still had cancer? Fuck! How was I going to wait until July for the results?* Another voice in my head yelled, "Shut up Holly and drink your fucking margarita!" Did I mention, I hadn't had a drink since last November and I deserved to celebrate. My second surgery was scheduled in six weeks and I would experience the pain, discomfort and the loss of my arms again. I pleaded with myself to stop worrying. I had done all of the right things and I deserved to enjoy my husband and the down time that came with that margarita. Wiley was relieved that chemo was over and I owed it to him too. I would be back in the medical soap opera of my life soon enough and I needed to just relax.

The very next day, I received the results from my last weekly CBC blood test and the numbers were perfect. NO more chemo, NO more weekly blood tests, and NO more awful shots in the stomach. With the double mastectomy and chemotherapy behind me, I looked forward to breast reconstruction. I had been through so much in such a short space of time, only five months since diagnosis, but sometimes it felt like a lifetime.

During my short medical break, Kathy at The Lavender Inn, invited us all back to her hotel for lunch. I joined the ladies I had met in January for our first reunion. It was nice to be back together supporting each other even just for the afternoon and we had developed supportive friendships over the last four months. Martina and I spoke on the phone and got together several times to visit or to ride our bicycles for an ice cream cone. Nicole, Jessi, and I followed each other on social media and kept in touch that way. Angela and I discovered we lived in the same neighborhood, and we walked together in the evening a couple times. It didn't matter what type of cancer we each had, they understood me more than anyone else because they were living it too. I will always be glad that I told everyone that I had breast cancer because it opened doors and created friendships. The *INNcourage* women were one of the silver linings of my breast cancer.

Martina, Holly, Nicole, Jessi and Angela back at The Lavender Inn for lunch and to catch up.

Chapter Four: Practical Suggestions

- Ask your oncologist about an anti-nausea patch before under-going treatment. You put the patch on your arm the night before treatment and leave on for three days.
- Enlist close friends and family members to help. Loved ones often feel helpless and want to be of service. Ask for help with meals, errands, housecleaning, and more.
- Communicate what foods you can eat and ask for help if you are not feeling up to shopping for groceries or cooking.
- Take a probiotic daily to help boost your compromised gut bacteria during chemo. Probiotics have been shown to be helpful to the body after taking any antibiotics as well.
- Constipation is a constant battle for some during surgeries and chemo. Prune juice, Metamucil, and stool softeners help.
- You are your own best advocate and nobody knows you or your body better. If you are having a reaction to a medicine, don't try and push through it. Tell your oncologist and see if there is an alternative or something that will make the symptoms better. Stand up for yourself.
- Buy adult coloring books and colorful felt pens to keep yourself busy.
- Ask other cancer survivors for their advice.
- If you haven't already, contact a cancer support center for information and ideas.
- Consider medical cannabis to help manage pain and nausea. Check with your oncologist and find out the laws in your area.
- Take time to start planning out some fun things to do when chemo is over to refocus and start enjoying your life again. No matter what happens, you have to be positive and keep looking forward to better times.
- Call in favors with your support group to help give your caregiver a break.

Chapter Five
Breast Tissue Expanders
May 18, 2016

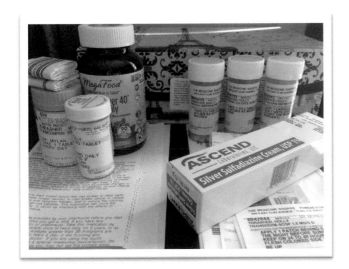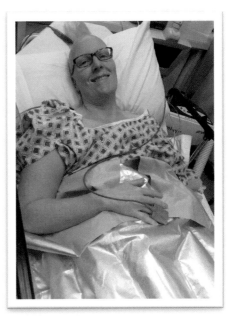

A whole lot of medication for before and after surgery. Warming up before surgery with a space blanket.

I was ready to begin breast reconstruction and that would include two more surgeries. After the double mastectomy, there was not enough skin or tissue left to accommodate breast implants. Tissue expanders needed to be inserted to expand the muscle and tissue to the point that implants would be able to be placed in my chest at a later date. Dr. Bern would use the same incisions that Dr. Rayhrer originally created during the double mastectomy surgery. He would open me back up and place the expanders behind my chest muscles, which would create a pocket for the future implants. Once the tissue expanders were in and the scars healed, he would fill them with saline every two weeks until they were at capacity.

The process would take three to six months depending on how much saline he put into the expanders at each appointment. I had talked to several other women that had gone through the process and one said that it took six months because it was very painful each time they were expanded. Summer was around the corner and expansion was all I had on the calendar.

My tissue expander surgery went as planned and only took a couple of hours. It was a lot less intense than the double mastectomy surgery. It was done at the outpatient Same Day Surgery center at our local hospital. After recovering for a couple hours, I was dressed and Wiley drove me back home to Ojai. I was groggy but felt good. The pain medicine kept me from feeling much of anything.

Once again, I had drains that came out of each breast, but Dr. Bern reassured me that they would be removed much faster than they had with the mastectomy. I returned the very next day for a follow up, but they were not done draining and I would have to wait another day. I arrived back at his office two days after surgery and the drains were removed. I remembered from the previous drain removals that after he had removed the stitches I needed to take a deep breath and relax while he gave the tubing a good yank. There was so much tubing and it was uncomfortable when it was removed, but it felt much better without it coiled up under my skin and tissue.

They gave me a tube of Silvadene® (silver sulfamide) cream that I had to apply to my stitches twice a day to prevent infection. I experienced pain for the first couple days and then it became more tolerable. I was able to stop the pain medication after two days which allowed me to avoid the constipation that came with opioids. The following week, I was back for another follow up appointment and for Dr. Bern to check my healing and stitches. The stitches looked good, but it was still too early to remove them.

My tissue expanders were similar to implants but they were just temporary and had a purpose. They had a self-sealing, magnetic, internal port to make the fill-ups a breeze. Dr. Bern had done my first fill up while I was under anesthesia. He had put 130 CCs of saline into each of the expanders, so when I woke up, I had more breast than I had since they were completely removed. My clothes fit again. The stitches were not the most comfortable and I wore very soft clothes that kept the fabric from rubbing.

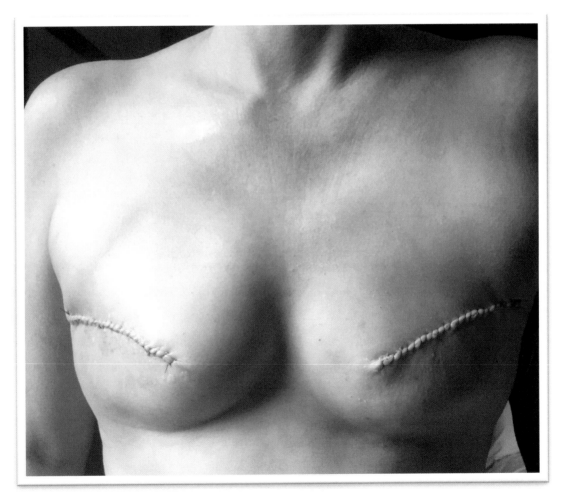

Tissue expanders were in and I had my first fill up during surgery.

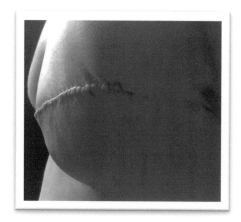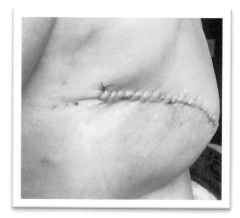

The left and right incisions were stitched up tightly while they healed and resembled licorice twists.

Tamoxifen® Sucks!
May 25, 2016

Due to the hormonal nature of my breast cancer, ER+ (Estrogen receptor positive) PR+ (progesterone receptor positive) it was recommended that I begin taking Tamoxifen® to further eliminate the estrogen production in my body. Tamoxifen® was a SERM or selective estrogen receptor modulator. It would act by blocking estrogen from attaching to the estrogen receptors on my cancer cells. It would slow the growth of tumors and kill tumor cells.[vii] It had been in use for over 40 years and would reduce the chances of my breast cancer from reoccurring, so we had try it.

The Tamoxifen® leaflet described the most common side effects which included menopausal symptoms like hot flashes, vaginal dryness, low libido, mood swings, and nausea. I already had the hot flashes and probably the mood swings. *How bad could it be?* It was the list of rare side effects in the pamphlet that concerned me; anxiety, skin blistering, skin peeling, or loosening of the skin and mucous membranes, blurred vision, cataracts in the eyes or other eye problems, change in vaginal discharge, chest pain, chills and confusion.[viii] *Wow. That didn't sound fun.*

Since I was off all medications from the expander surgery it was time to try my first dose of Tamoxifen® and find out what it would be like to be on it for five to ten years. Due to my medication sensitivity, Dr. Shah decided I would start with a half dose until we knew how I tolerated it. Within twelve hours of my first half dose, my scalp was covered in small red bumps. I let her know the next morning but she had me continue half a dose for three days and then to try a full dose on the fourth day. After one week on the medication, my arms and legs were also covered with hives. Luckily, they didn't itch. She wanted me to continue the full dose in the hopes that my body would regulate. It didn't. After the second week, my whole body was covered in red, itchy, hives. I had them everywhere. My head, arms, legs, back and weirdly, inside my eyelids. I felt absolutely miserable. Benadryl® was one of the only ways to relieve the itchiness, but I hated the groggy, sleepy effects of it and it did not eliminate the hives, just made them more tolerable.

I was also experiencing a host of other awful symptoms. I had severe joint and muscle pain to the point where it was hard to walk after I was sitting. My knees, elbows and shoulders ached all the time and my leg bones hurt inside. The hot flashes became utterly unbearable. I kept a log of the hot flashes and I got one every single hour of every single day. I slept on a towel to keep the sheets dry. Insomnia kicked in and sleeping became impossible. I had overwhelming anxiety and felt like I was in someone else's body. I called Dr. Shah again and reported that my vision was blurry and I couldn't focus my eyes. I had a lot of the rare side effects described on the leaflet.

She had me stop Tamoxifen® for one week and overnight the hot flashes became more bearable and the hives started to go away. I assumed that I was done but she wanted me to try one quarter of the recommended dosage. She told me that she wanted to make sure that I gave it my best shot. It was the wonder drug that kept cancer away, so I reluctantly agreed. Within 24 hours of popping a quarter of the dose, small, red blister-like bumps appeared on my arms. They were not hives, they were blisters. It was very clear in that agonizing two and a half weeks that I was not going to be able to tolerate the medication at all. She had never heard of the skin blistering as a symptom, but I reminded her that it was on the leaflet, so she discontinued it completely. What a relief!

Tamoxifen® was the only option for me since I was considered premenopausal. I had only missed five periods and they wouldn't consider me menopausal until I had missed one full year of periods. Until then, there was no other anti-cancer drug option for a pre-menopausal woman like myself. I was happy that I couldn't tolerate it because quality of life was important, but I worried that my cancer would make a come-back without it. It was a dilemma that was totally out of my control.

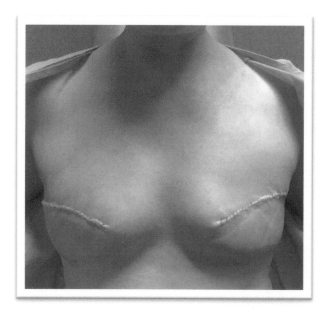

At my one week follow up, the bruising had turned a very unflattering yellow and
Dr. Bern said my stitches needed to remain in place another week.

Stitches Out, Please
May 31, 2016

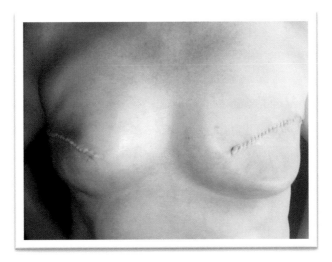

Dr. Bern removed the stitches very easily and with almost no discomfort.
The skin under the stitches remained red and sore while they healed with some bruising.

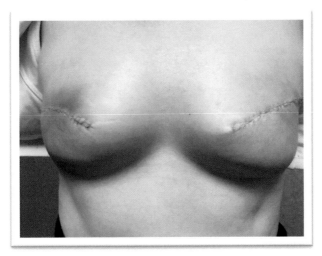

Lymphedema
June 6, 2016

While I waited patiently for the process to continue, I began to swim to regain my arm strength and mobility. I had not exercised since before my mastectomy in December, six months prior and I felt out of shape. The first time I got into the pool I flailed about trying to propel my body forward in the water with no luck. My arm muscles had atrophied and were too tight to move my arms over my head in the motion needed to propel myself through the water. *Great. I can't even swim*. I was pretty shocked as I envisioned myself gracefully gliding through the water without any problems. Wrong. I had to tread water to avoid the shooting pain that would radiate out from my underarm. I swam for five minutes that day. The next day, another five minutes and the third day I swam for ten minutes. I increased my laps over time to 30 minutes day. It was a much slower process than I realized, but I wanted to begin the process of losing all of the biscuit and mashed potato weight I had gained during chemo. I became very supportive of my own healing and didn't want to push my body too much but exercise felt good. I struggled with my arms but didn't know what else to do.

One day I was at our local athletic club ready for a swim, when I bumped into my friend Renee, a cancer survivor and Assistant Director at Ojai Cares. She looked me up and down and had me hold out my arms. I thought it was a little odd at the time, but trusted her instinct. She said, "Holly, your left arm is swollen and it appears you have lymphedema. Are you in physical therapy?" My arms were sore and ached and I assumed it was a result of the swimming I had been doing. I had seen my primary care physician, a radiologist, a surgeon, an oncologist, a dermatologist, a plastic surgeon, a cardiologist, a genetic counselor, and been through two surgeries, and nobody mentioned physical therapy. Not a single one of my doctors had looked closely at my arms and nobody noticed there was a problem developing. My arms weren't causing me extreme pain, so the mild discomfort of lymphedema went unnoticed.

Thank goodness for Renee's sharp eye and experience, she caught it early. I contacted my oncologist and told her that my left arm was swollen and I needed physical therapy. No problem. *Really?*

Fill'er Up!
June 10, 2016

Dr. Bern filled each expander with 130 CCs of saline during my surgery which began the expansion process. There would be a series of fill appointments to further expand out my skin and tissue. Each fill appointment added another 130 CCs of saline to each expander. I felt nothing for the first hour, but after the local anesthesia wore off both breasts ached and were sore for a couple days. By the third day, most of the discomfort was gone. The more saline he put in at each fill meant less needle sticks, less office visits, and less time with the expanders.

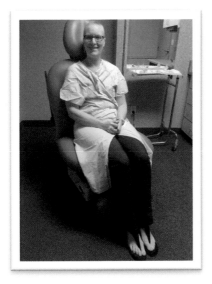

My hair had started to grow back after chemo. What a huge relief, being bald was not a self-esteem booster.

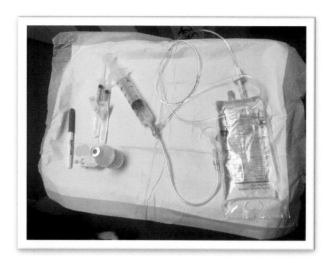

Tray set up with everything Dr. Bern needed to fill my expanders; A magnet and Sharpie to mark the location of the ports, a needle and lidocaine to numb the area, and a syringe with saline to expand my breasts.

Tissue expander fill process:

1. Dr. Bern found the port using a magnet.

2. Marked the spot on the breast with a Sharpie where the needle would be inserted.

3. Filled the syringe with 130 CCs of saline

4. Wiped my breast with alcohol to disinfect

5. Local anesthetic applied to the area with a couple of needle sticks

6. Dr. Bern carefully inserted the needle through my skin and into the port

7. Filled the tissue expander with the saline

8. Cleaned the blood from the needle stick and put a band aid on it

9. After the needle was removed, the material in the port resealed on its own to prevent leaks

10. Repeat on the other breast

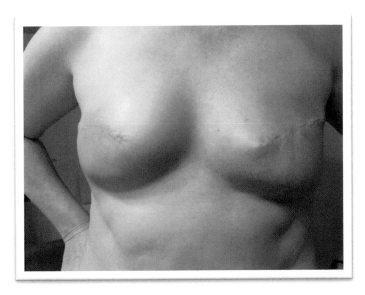

Before and after: We had waited three weeks to allow the stitches to heal so they could endure more saline in a second fill. The band aids covered the spots where the needle was inserted through the ports.

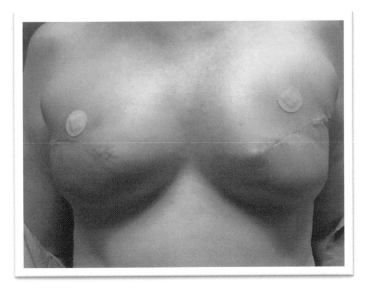

Looking Kind of Like Breasts
June 13, 2016

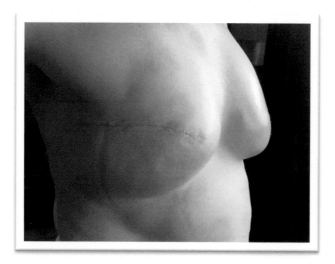

Since they were tissue expanders, they were not the same shape as breast implants. They felt and looked a little odd. Their purpose was to expand my skin, tissue, and muscle so they could be replaced with real implants.

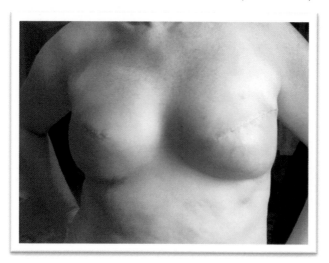

Third Fill
June 24, 2016

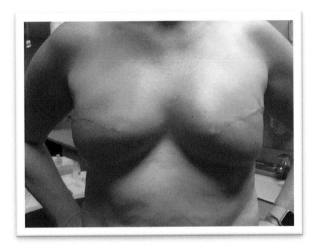

Before: The third fill was much easier than the last because I knew exactly what to expect.

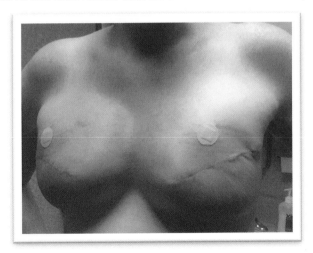

After: The grey in the photo was not bruising, the Sharpie marks that Dr. Bern made to locate the ports had smeared after alcohol was rubbed on the area.

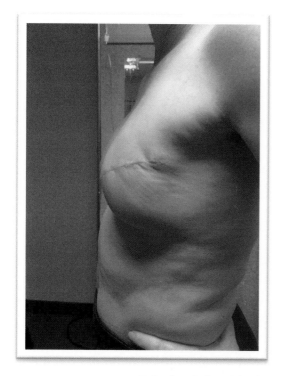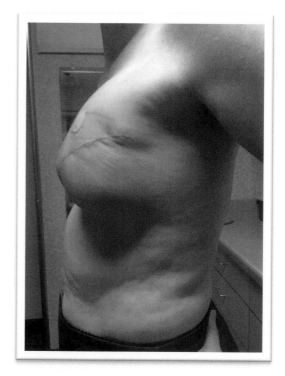

Before and after side view of third fill. There was a definite difference.
My breasts were sore for about two to three days after each fill.

Independence Day
July 2, 2016

It had been six whole months since we had closed the candy store and I never missed the business itself because it took 50-60 hours a week of my time, but I really missed my employees and customers. I desperately needed a party, so, we invited some close friends and our "adopted daughters without all of the paperwork" to celebrate the Fourth of July at our house. The weeks that led up to the party were occupied with cleaning the backyard, gluing our old Kingston's store front sign to a wood board, painting, and planning. It felt good to be alive and active again. Our Fourth of July party allowed me to thank everyone for all of their love and support during the previous eight months of cancer drama. Hard to believe it had been eight months already.

I had a thin layer of hair, my eyelashes and eyebrows had partially grown back in, and my energy level increased weekly. I still wasn't able to wear makeup because my face and eyes would swell from the chemical sensitivity I had developed from chemo. My nose had also become hyper sensitive to any kind of perfumes or scented products. I knew that it would take about a year until I felt like myself again, at least that's what I had heard from other chemo survivors. In the meantime, I was just trying to process everything that had happened.

Chelsi, Hannah, Holly, Alexis, and Lucia reunited to celebrate Fourth of July
at my house in Ojai. I love these young ladies so much!

No Evidence
July 5, 2016

  The Tuesday after Fourth of July weekend I showed up at my oncologist's office for the results of my first tumor marker test. I had made the appointment three months before at the end of my chemo. I wanted to be cancer-free but found out that designation would not be considered until my five-year mark. Instead, if my blood test results had a score of 32 or less, I would have the new title, *no evidence of cancer*. I nervously paced the waiting room while Wiley fidgeted with his phone. I needed the results ASAP. *What if my tumor markers were over 32? Would more chemo be ordered? I couldn't fathom it.*

After what seemed like days, a nurse escorted Wiley and I into the familiar room. My eyes darted from the terrible 1980's Broadway themed paintings on the wall, to the floor, the chair, and the small sign on the wall that I read every time I was placed in that room;

"Cancer is so limited, it cannot cripple Love, it cannot shatter Hope, it cannot diminish Faith,

it cannot destroy Peace, it cannot kill Friendship, it cannot suppress Memories, it cannot silence

Courage, it cannot invade the Soul, it cannot steal Eternal Life, it cannot conquer the spirit."

Ha. That day I was over it. Yes. It actually could do all of those things and if I didn't find out the results of the test soon, I was also going to go bat-shit CRAZY and yes, cancer could cause CRAZINESS! Put that on your stupid fucking sign. Just as I contemplated ripping the sign off the wall and throwing it in the trash can, the door opened. Thank goodness Dr. Shah didn't make me wait long today. I'd lost it. She came straight to the point. "Your numbers are good and there is NO EVIDENCE OF CANCER!" Wiley and I both let out big sighs of relief and I felt bad for letting cancer limit my thinking. My shoulders relaxed, my stomach unclenched, and I couldn't stop smiling. Wiley was smiling too. His brow unfurled and he looked like he had just had an awesome hour-long massage. All the tension was gone. When we walked out of the office that day it felt like we had just won the lottery. Euphoria and giddiness overcame us, we held hands on the way to the car and it was like being in love for the first time.

I was FREE. No evidence of cancer, meant no evidence of disease in the medical world. My score that day for the tumor marker test also known as CA 15-3 was 16. That was half of what it could have been and so it was considered very low and promising. As good as the news was, I wasn't off the hook yet. We still needed to find out if I was menopausal and then reduce my hormones with an anti-cancer drug. I asked if I would be able to avoid medication with ovary removal surgery, but I was told that I needed to try the meds first since removal would not eliminate all of my hormones.

My choice of drug after menopause was Exemestane® (Aromasin®), it was part of a class of drugs called aromatase inhibitors. They had far fewer side effects than Tamoxifen® and most women tolerated them better. Exemestane® was used to treat several different types of breast cancer including the hormone receptor positive breast cancer that I had. It would inhibit the growth of estrogen, but the downside of aromatase inhibitors included possible heart problems and osteoporosis.[ix] I asked if that was really a better option and was told that compared to cancer it was. Dr. Shah gave me a prescription for Exemestane® and referred me to a gynecologist to test my hormones. If I was in menopause I was supposed to start the prescription immediately.

Fourth Fill
July 8, 2016

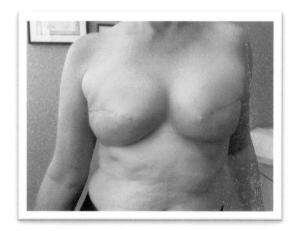 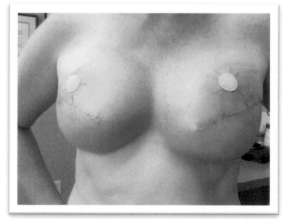

Before and after fourth fill. Holy crap they were getting big!

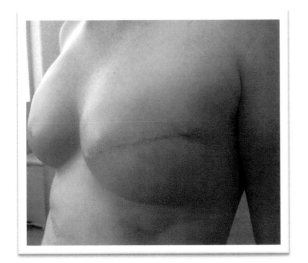
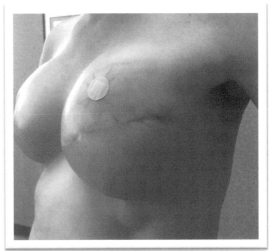

Left breast, before and after fourth fill. Wow!

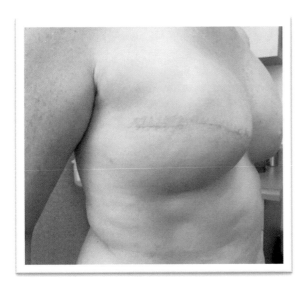
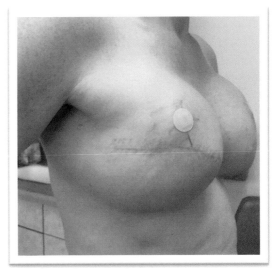

Right breast before and after fourth fill. Va-Va-Voom!

Physical Therapy
July 25, 2016

I was healed from the breast implant surgery and my expansion was going quickly. My arms and the muscles in my neck and back needed help. I was approved by my insurance for eight sessions of physical therapy. I met with Joanna Schindel, a physical therapist at Swanner Physical Therapy in Ojai. My first appointment was a consultation to determine where my arms were at in terms of ability and what was needed to improve them. I paid a $20 copay for each session and it proved to be worth every penny.

At my first PT appointment Joanna measured my arms at different points to track my progress and to help detect swelling. My left arm was in need of the most attention. It was the arm that had three lymph nodes taken out where the cancer had been. My left arm was only a little swollen compared to the right arm which appeared fine in comparison. Joanna taught me how to manually drain my arms every evening or when needed with lymphatic massage. She also developed an exercise program to gently target the muscles in my arms to help strengthen them while reducing the swelling. After a couple weeks of physical therapy, I felt results. I no longer flapped my arms around in the water like a fish on a hook and I could swim laps with my arms dedicated to the task. I saw Joanna several times before my final breast implant surgery and we postponed future physical therapy treatments until Dr. Bern gave me the green light to return.

Alternative Therapies

There are so many different alternative therapies being used in conjunction with cancer treatments here in the US. They provide pain relief, relaxation, and benefit healing. The downside is the cost. Insurance does not cover most of the therapies, so you will pay the total amount out of pocket. Some of the therapies are offered free at local cancer centers and hospitals. Here are a few alternative therapies that I used during my treatment.

- Manual Lymphatic Drainage: Light massage to encourage natural drainage of lymph from the tissues back toward the heart. Not covered by insurance.
- Oncology Massage: Uses existing massage techniques in a safe way to avoid complications of cancer and cancer treatment. Not covered by insurance, but available at cancer centers for free.
- Myofascial Release Massage: A type of physical therapy that targets the tissues that surround and support the muscles in your body. Not covered by insurance.
- Reiki Healing: Originated in Japan and is a safe, natural method of spiritual energy healing used to counteract the effects of chemotherapy, surgery, and depression. Not covered by insurance, but available at cancer centers for free.
- Guided Imagery: A trained practitioner helps you use your imagination along with breathing exercises to reach a state of emotional calm and deep relaxation. Not covered by insurance, but available at cancer centers for free.
- Acupuncture: A component of Chinese medicine that stimulates specific points on the body by inserting thin needles gently into the skin. Some insurance companies will pay for treatment and you are only responsible for the cost of your copay.
- Cannabis: Uses the whole unprocessed plant or its basic extracts to treat symptoms of illness. It has shown positive results with controlling pain and nausea during cancer treatments and surgeries. Not covered by insurance.

Water Balloons
August 2, 2016

My life previously had been occupied with non-stop activity, seven days a week. The stress of breast cancer along with the multiple surgeries and intensity of chemo altered my eating habits, metabolism, activity levels, and my body. I no longer looked the part of a lean, woman living a healthy California lifestyle. The gut around my middle had expanded and nothing fit. In an effort to try to regain my body, Wiley and I continued to swim at the club, but I was surprised to find that my arms, legs, and stomach didn't seem to shrink like I thought they would.

My breasts in their original form had been sort of round, slightly droopy from the natural effects of gravity, and very soft and pliable. After expanders were inserted they were very round, higher up, and not as naturally soft. The saline sloshed about inside the silicone shell of the expanders and we started referring to my breasts as water balloons. Not exactly the nickname you'd want, but it was true and we had more than one good laugh about them. The saline implants did not feel as realistic as the silicone implants I had felt during my original consultation appointment. I wanted my new breasts to feel as real as possible and decided I wanted to go with silicone instead. I also began to wonder if they were too big. They felt like they were really high up under my chin. The metal ports that were part of their design had begun to put more and more pressure on the inside of my breast tissue as they were expanded.

At my last fill appointment, I let Dr. Bern know I had changed my mind about having saline implants. With that decision made, he handed each of us a different silicone implant and told us we needed to choose an implant size. We held the implants in our hands and he explained that I could choose an implant size from 525 CCs all the way up to 650 CCs. After the fifth and final fill, my expanders were at 650 CCs of saline and they felt huge.

With my new, larger body the bigger implants would be fine, but I wasn't exactly thrilled with all of the mash potato, full fat butter, and warm biscuit weight staying put. Holding an implant in your hand and then trying to visualize it under your skin was not an easy task. I wanted a size C cup, not a D cup. Dr. Bern explained there was no real way to compare my idea of cup size with CCs since every bra size was different. I had to go with my gut and opted for 560 CCs. It was right in the middle of the sizes he thought would be best. He didn't want me to regret not going bigger, but I didn't share those concerns. I was more concerned that I would wake up after surgery and regret such large breasts. Either way, 560 CCs was bigger than I was before. *How could I go wrong?* If I remember correctly, Wiley thought 650 would be just right. *Of course, he did!*

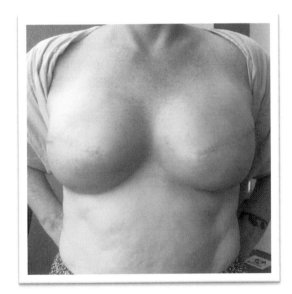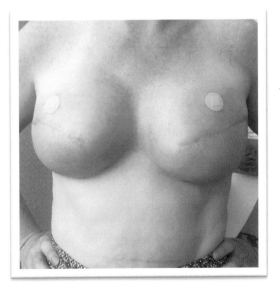

Before and after, fifth and final fill.

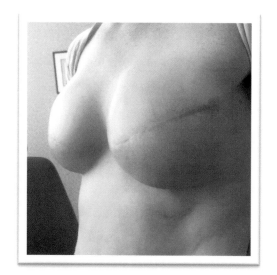 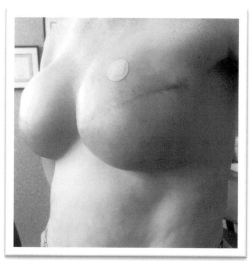

Left breast, before and after fifth and final fill. 650 CCs in each breast.

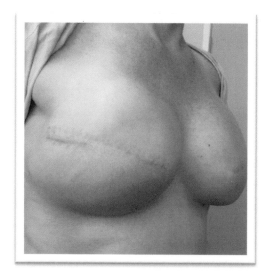 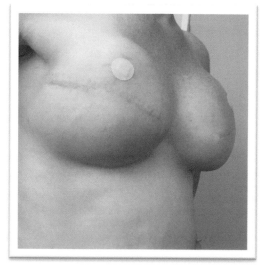

Right breast, before and after. No more fills. Hurray!

Less than two weeks from surgery, I woke up in the middle of the night in a complete panic. The 560 CC implants I had chosen were going to be way too big for me. I called Dr. Bern's office the next morning and instructed them to purchase 525 CC implants for me instead. 525 CCs was the smallest that he had recommended.

At my pre-op appointment, Dr. Bern confirmed one more time that I did not want nipple reconstruction done during the implant surgery. In order to make them he would have to remove skin from my thighs leaving scars, then form that skin into a small nipple, and then sew it onto my breast. A tattoo artist would tattoo the areola and color it in with tattoo ink to look like a nipple. The other option was to skip the sewn-on nipple and have a 3-D nipple tattooed onto each breast. After my own nipples were removed I knew that I didn't want them replaced. I had come to terms with their absence. *No nipples for me!*

I wanted art on my breasts. Soft, pink, Japanese style cherry blossoms tattooed to cover the scars and mimic nipples. Most women wanted nipples in one form or another, I was not the norm, but I didn't care. It was for me and not anyone else. Well, that's not entirely true. It did help that Wiley loved the idea of my tattoos and understood how I felt about it. With all of the details ironed out, we booked my implant surgery for August 17th, 2016, two weeks away.

Fiesta Fun
August 5, 2016

I decided that my breasts and I had been through a lot and deserved a little positive attention for once. I bought a dress with a plunging neckline and Wiley and I went out dancing with our friends in Santa Barbara for the city's annual Fiesta celebration. I put on a little make up and I had enough hair to appear as if nothing had happened. There were dozens of friends and well-wishers concerned about me and my breasts. I didn't consider them mine, since they were just expanders and being removed soon, so I let all of my curious friends touch them. Funny thing was, I felt nothing. The nerves that surrounded my scars had not regenerated and they felt numb. Wiley was a good sport and smiled and laughed at me. By the way, I wasn't drinking alcohol at all with the surgery in my near future, so nothing inappropriate happened, just a lot of giggles. I was surprised to find a lot of my friends, both male and female, did not know what saline filled breasts felt like. All in the name of education.

My close friend Melissa, myself, Wiley, and my sister, Sarah, celebrating Fiesta with friends before my implant surgery.

Chapter Five: Practical Suggestions

- Always take someone with you to every doctor's appointment. It helps to remember what was said and you might need the extra support if you get bad news.

- Ask about other options to the pharmaceuticals or surgeries being recommended.

- Talk to other breast cancer survivors to find out what they did and how they feel about their choices. It will help you get perspective on your choices.

- You don't have to choose reconstruction if it doesn't resonate with you. Go with what feels natural for you.

- Use the meds if you need them and don't be a hero if you have pain, but be careful not to abuse them either.

- If you are having an adverse reaction to a medication, report it immediately.

- Are there alternative therapies that would complement your treatment? Ask around.

- I know I keep harping on it, but if you haven't gone to a cancer support center...find one and go! The support is priceless.

- If you have had surgery, an injury or a physical problem that needs fixing, ask your doctor today if PT will help you. It helped me immensely.

- Be gentle with yourself. This is a long road, so try not to be too critical of your looks and body.

- Follow your inner voice when making decisions. Don't let anyone sway what you know to be the right decision. This is your life and your body.

- If you are up to it, have some fun.

Chapter Six
Final Breast Implant Surgery
August 17, 2016

I was so eager to have my awkward tissue expanders and their very uncomfortable metal ports removed and replaced. Right before they wheeled me into my final reconstruction surgery, Dr. Bern whipped out his set of colorful Sharpie pens. He made himself a road map of sorts right on my chest. I couldn't resist a good laugh and Wiley got the photo. The 525 written in the center of my chest was the size of the breast implants I had chosen. He had ordered several sizes just in case I had a last-minute change of heart, but 525 CCs was the magic number.

I had developed a swollen, puffy area above each arm pit called a seroma and Dr. Bern wanted to remove them during surgery. He drew bulls-eyes on the skin just above my underarms to show where he would remove the seromas with liposuction. A seroma seemed like a place you would go for a vacation and a good glass of wine, not a weird bulge. Wishful thinking on my part. My seromas were described as pockets of clear fluid that had developed as a result of previous surgeries and would not go away on their own.

I made the mistake of watching a video online that showed a liposuction procedure. I watched a liposuction rod plunge in and out of a woman's stomach area. It sucked up her blobby, gelatinous fat like a vacuum cleaner and deposited it into a clear glass container. It was awful, but Dr. Bern told me that it was the best way to remove the fluid and the fatty tissue. He said it would be included in my surgery at no extra charge. I had to ask as I didn't want to end up with a surprise lipo bill. Insurance was paying, so I agreed to the free liposuction and tried to erase the images of the video from my brain.

The vertical lines drawn on the top and bottom of my breasts would show Dr. Bern where the implants should be placed. I had voiced concern about resembling a porn star and didn't want the breast implants too high up. He promised he would make them look natural. The "save" written on my inner breasts reminded him that the little bit of original breast tissue that Dr. Rayhrer had saved needed to be preserved. The tissue kept around the implant would help them look more natural. I feared breast implants that looked like fake, oversized melons that barely moved. I didn't want them to enter a room before I did.

The last of Dr. Bern's Sharpie breast-road-map, showed dotted lines down the middle of my breasts, that led toward leaf shapes at the end of my scars. He was going to use the same scars that had been opened up twice before, but he was going to open me up farther back toward my arm pits. He was not going to open the scars end to end like the first two surgeries. The leaf shape was a bit of skin that had puckered slightly during healing. The excess skin would be removed and the area smoothed out.

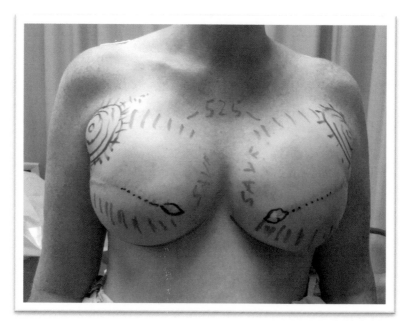

One-of-a-kind pre-surgery artwork by my plastic surgeon, Dr. Samuel Bern.

110

So far, that was the easiest of the three surgeries. Partially because I now had two behind me and felt comfortable going under the knife. The surgery lasted a few hours and recovery was quick. I was up and out of the hospital bed before I knew it. Wiley loaded me into the car and situated a set of seatbelt pillows just over my abdomen and pelvis that kept the seatbelt from pressing on my stitches. I was not allowed to lift my arms and had drains that stuck out of both breasts again.

I was the new, proud owner of silicone breast implants. I had been wound up so much with gauze and tape that I couldn't even peek at them. We joked that I looked like the heroic female lead character in the latest *Star Wars* movie. I was told to rest overnight for the twenty-minute trip back to Dr. Bern the next day. It was a bit like those cheesy reality TV shows when they hype the unveiling of the new you. I eagerly waited for the big reveal and hoped the drains would also be removed. What a wild ride. I had gone from breasts to no breasts and back again.

All wrapped up with my drains peeking out from the bottom of the bandages.

These are Mine
August 20, 2016

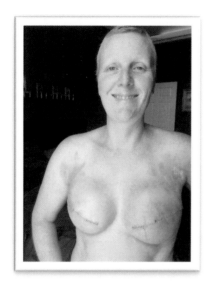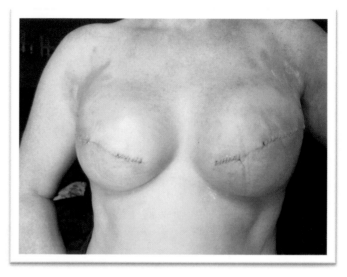

Bruised and battered but I was happy. I like to tell people, "I'm just glad to be here."
I stole that line from a dear friend of ours, Pete Thorsen, and it was true.

I was done with all of my scheduled surgeries and eager for the stitches to be removed. According to Dr. Bern, my silicone implants would be good for seven to ten years and I would need them removed before twelve years. After the implants had been placed they would be considered cosmetic and it would be on my dime the next time they needed to be replaced. That bothered me because breast cancer which resulted in a double mastectomy and reconstruction with silicone breast implants was not my fault or elective. It seemed like insurance should pay to replace them especially since there might be complications due to the fact that they were placed after breast reconstruction. Oh well, I should probably start saving up for it now.

In the meantime, Dr. Bern recommended I have either a breast MRI or breast ultrasound every year to check the surrounding tissue for possible tumors and to make sure the implants had not leaked. Saline implants could rupture and immediately deflate like a tire, hence the term, flat tire. Silicone implants on the other hand could slowly leak silicone gel into my body without anyone aware it was happening.

In my case, a breast MRI was out of the question because of the titanium and nickel device that was implanted in my heart. MRI machines use a very large magnet for imaging, and since there was metal in my heart, no MRI's for me. Ultrasound was safer and the best way to safeguard my implants and heart.

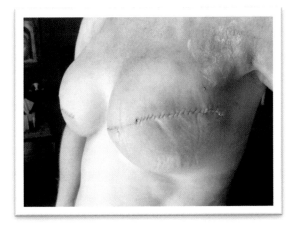 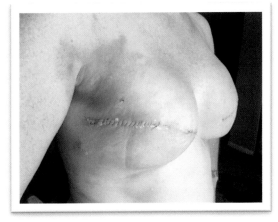

The skin and tissue above my armpits where the liposuction rod went in and out was bumpy, raw, and inflamed. Even the slightest touch made me wince. I covered the area with Silvadene® cream but the bruising and tenderness lasted for weeks. As the area healed, the bruising moved down into my arms and resembled a hematoma. I phoned Alicia, because I knew that she would be able to help me with the healing. Alicia gently moved the lymph in my arms and chest with a combination of myofascial release and lymphatic massage. After a ninety-minute appointment the bruising had significantly dissipated.

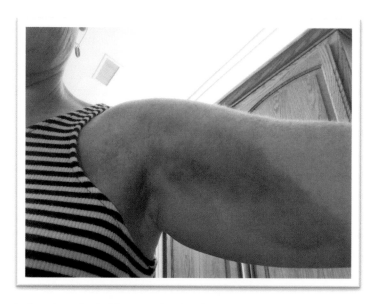

(Top) Bruising before Lymphatic Massage. (Bottom) Bruising 24 hours After Lymphatic Massage.

In Stitches
August 26, 2016

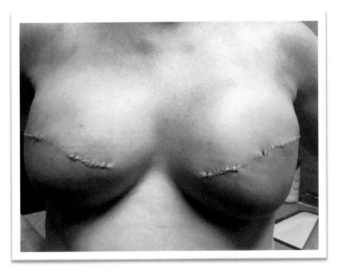

There was a small space where my nipples used to be that was not opened up in this surgery.

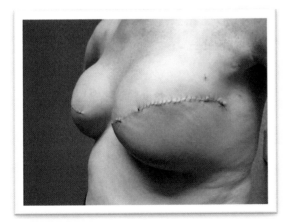
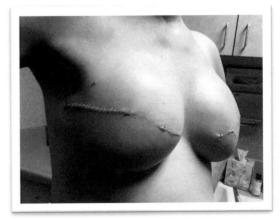

Left and right breasts before stitches were removed. There was some bruising that was still not healed.

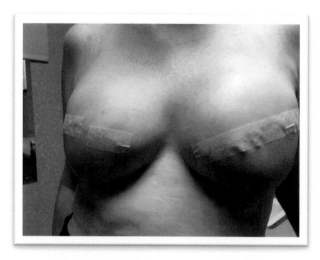

The stitches were removed with little to no discomfort. The fabric tape was to remain on the scars until my next appointment or until they fell off.

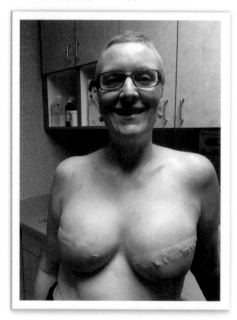

May I Introduce My New Breasts
September 8, 2016
276 days since double mastectomy (9 months 1 day)

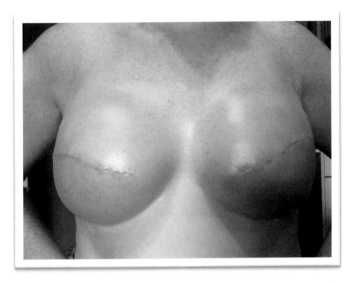

The right breast scar seemed to be healing faster and was a lot less sore than the left.

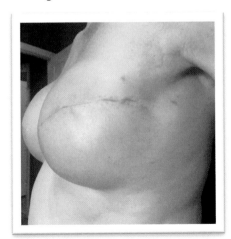 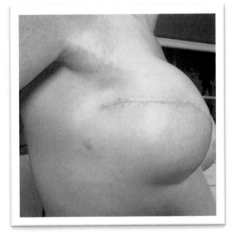

My breasts constantly changed for nine months and I had forgotten that it would end. When I looked in the mirror and saw my breasts, it had been four weeks since the final implant surgery and two weeks since the stitches were removed. They were mine. The awful and uncomfortable saline tissue expanders had been removed and replaced with silicone implants. The implants felt softer and much more like actual breast tissue compared to the water balloon saline expanders. I wasn't ready to start liking them and didn't want Wiley to touch them yet as they were still a little tender to the touch.

How could I love these big, fake breasts when I had loved my original ones? I think I still had more grieving to do before I could start to like them or contemplate loving them. I felt like I was betraying my own body by accepting what felt like porn star sex symbols. The reality was, my own breasts had tried to kill me and they were long gone. My new breasts would never try to do that to me and I had to start the process of accepting them sooner or later.

I started to touch them and let Wiley touch them too. Some days, they felt like they weren't part of me. Just two big mounds sticking out from my chest. Whenever I leaned over, the silicone implants felt like they were sliding up my chest toward my neck. It was all too new and there was still a lot of healing to be done before I could or would accept them as my own. *I wondered when that would happen or if that would ever happen.* Oh well, another bridge to cross sometime in the future. I kept adding more and more bridges to cross. I could travel across the globe from one bridge to the next escaping the reality I was living, if only they had been real.

Three weeks after surgery Dr. Bern cleared me for exercise and I started physical therapy with Joanna again to strengthen my arm muscles. It was easier but no less challenging. I swam a couple days a week which helped immensely. The hot flashes that resulted from my sudden introduction to menopause still gripped me. I had researched the many Chinese Herbs that were touted for menopause symptoms. Licorice root, milk thistle, Dang Gui, Ginseng, and black cohosh were recommended. Unfortunately, the majority of the herbs were considered estrogenic in nature, the reason why they worked well to relieve symptoms. Estrogenic meant that they mimicked the hormone estrogen and my estrogen dominant breast cancer was at risk if I used those compounds. No Chinese herbs for me.

In desperation to find something, anything that would relieve the oppressive hot flashes, I tried acupuncture. The sessions were available to me for a $20 copay and I was allowed 20 sessions a year with my insurance. The treatment itself was relaxing, stimulating, and I felt like I was melting into the table. I was sure that I had found relief but on the drive home from my first appointment my head started to pound. I had a severe migraine headache that lasted all evening and kept me in bed overnight. The acupuncturist and I decided that it was a fluke, so I went for a second and third treatment. A severe migraine was the result of each treatment. My acupuncturist did some research and found that a very small percentage of people, almost nobody, experienced that reaction. *Lucky me.* At the recommendation of the acupuncturist and my oncologist I gave up on Chinese acupuncture. *I don't want my acupuncture results to deter you from trying it, because every single person that I know that tried it, benefitted.*

Tumor Time
October 4, 2016

I wondered what my parents would think had they been alive. *Would they accept it and be supportive or would they encourage me to ignore medical treatment and only pray?* I believed that my mom would place her hand on my back, like she had so many times since my childhood, and gently rub all the worry away without speaking of any of it. My dad would go on as if nothing had happened and talk to me about politics, people and life, while giving me back my sense of peace. I missed both of them so much.

Three months passed in the blink of an eye and I was back in my oncologist's office for the results of my second quarterly tumor marker test. Again, the fear and uncertainty swirled around the magic number that would be presented to me. *If the results of the CA 15-3 blood test were 16 last time, what would they be now? Would it be more or less? Was I still healthy and free of cancer?* Dr. Shah entered the room and immediately informed Wiley and I that my numbers had dropped again from 16 to a low 14. I asked if they would ever go to 0 and she said they would not but any number under 32 was considered acceptable. *Why don't tumor markers go back to 0 if you no longer have cancer?* I was told that the protein used to detect cancer in my cells would naturally produce small amounts in my body even if my cancer was not active. There would always be some amount of the protein detected with or without cancer. Dr. Shah suggested I continue to follow up with her every three months to check my tumor markers. Some patients chose not to check their tumor markers at all. I thought that was crazy but she explained that for some survivors it was just too stressful. I believed that knowledge was power and I told her that I wanted to know if my cancer came back so I had a choice in what I would do about it. She encouraged me to exercise regularly and move on with my life.

When I was a kid, I took tap dancing classes and loved it. I couldn't remember why I stopped going, but as an adult, I had always dreamed of tapping again. I had been thinking about it a lot but hadn't wanted to drive out of town to go to a class. Out of the blue, I checked the newsletter for our athletic club and there it was, Beginning and Intermediate Tap Dancing classes for adults once a week. *Thank you, universe.* After I signed up I found out that my tap teacher's mom had died of breast cancer and there was another breast cancer survivor in our class. It was meant to be.

Stephanie Hull, my Tap teacher, referred to Tap as dementia prevention. One of the side effects of chemotherapy was chemo brain. I definitely felt it when I spoke. Sometimes it was hard to find words and it felt like my mouth and brain were disconnected. It also made movement labored at times, but I was determined to keep at it. I felt really frustrated after some classes but reminded myself that I was doing it for fun and not to take it too seriously. It took months for my brain to step up and translate the moves efficiently, but it finally did. Tap was good for both my legs and my brain and my movement no longer felt forced. It was exactly what I needed for healing my mind and body.

Looking Good
October 11, 2016

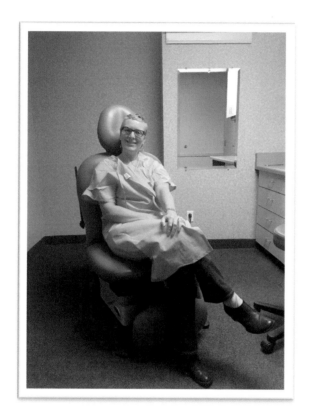

     This was my fifteenth appointment in ten months since my initial consultation last January. I wore the pink gown and bared my breasts once again for inspection. It had been nine weeks post implant surgery and I no longer felt pain on a regular basis. I did experience the occasional twinge that could be gently rubbed away. Whenever I felt a twinge, I would gently rub my breast round and round to relieve the discomfort. My face would tighten and I winced with discomfort until the twinge subsided and I relaxed out of the pain. I opened my eyes on several occasions to find I had been totally zoned out. I didn't even know my eyes were shut and that I was rubbing my breast in the middle of the grocery store. People probably thought I was out of my mind. I did that by accident a lot. I didn't really care that anyone else was around. Well, I did care but my acute discomfort took precedence over anyone else's judgement. I knew I could always pull the cancer card and that would explain why I needed to rub my breasts right there and then.

I complained that the area above my armpit was still tender and the tissue under the skin bumpy and uneven. Dr. Bern inspected the area and told me that it would take time to heal the bumpiness. He was pleased with my progress and asked me to return in two months. That would put our next appointment right before Christmas. In the meantime, I kept doing what I was doing. Every morning after I showered, I would rub Vitamin E oil into the scars, the areas around my arm pits, and my chest. I had been told to avoid soy due to the estrogenic effect of it and hadn't realized that most Vitamin E oil was made from soy. I was forced to find an alternative. After a bit of searching, I found a Vitamin E oil that was made from sunflower seeds with no estrogenic effect.

A lot of my breast cancer discoveries came from other cancer survivor's recommendations. In general, I found that my doctors did not suggest alternative treatments on their own. However, when I presented my doctors with alternative treatment ideas that I was interested in, like cannabis or lymphatic massage, I usually found they were supportive.

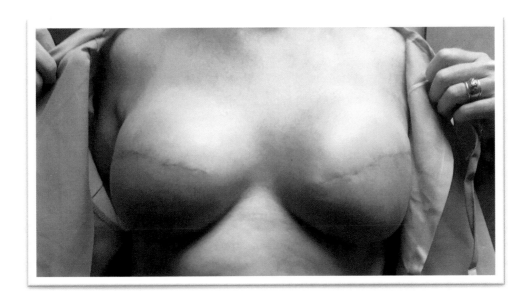

The scars healed very nicely in the center of my breasts, but almost two months post-surgery it was still sore on the left breast scar and had puckered the skin. The right breast scar was healing faster and no longer sore.

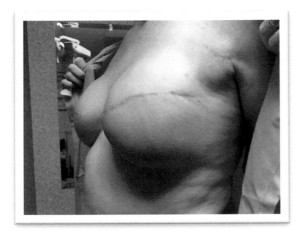 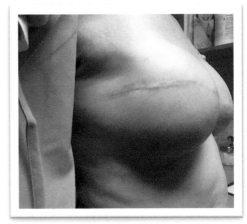

One Whole Year Since My Double Mastectomy
November 26, 2016

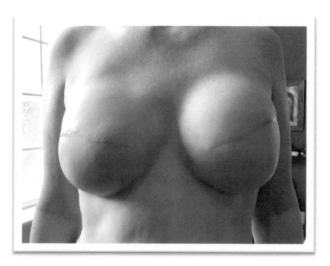

The scars continued to heal on the front of my breasts and I noticed the scars on the sides were thicker.

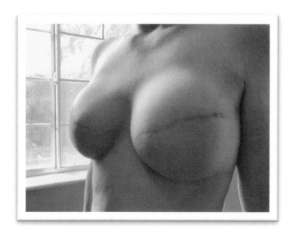 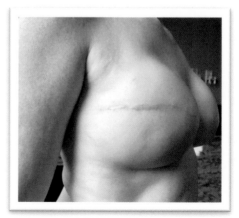

The left breast scar started to thicken and continued to be very pink and sore.

It was Thanksgiving once again. The year before I had been diagnosed only days before the holiday and was filled with trepidation and fear. This year I was alive, happy, and healing. I had always loved the holidays. My mom would plan the perfect table and meal for all of us to enjoy. She always bought the best, sparing no expense for our family holiday meals. The mood at my parents' home was relaxed and they never turned away any of our friends that wanted to join us.

We no longer got together as a family on Thanksgiving since we all had active lives and obligations. My mom was not around to entertain and bring us together, so we had let the Thanksgiving tradition fall by the wayside and instead got together at Christmas. Wiley, Vance, and I invented our own tradition which included our closest friends and some type of exotic cuisine. It reminded me of the scene in *The Christmas Story* movie after the dog ate the turkey and they went out for Chinese food. That year, Wiley's mom, Karen, and our close friends Jeff, David, and Sage joined us for our Thanksgiving adventure. It was really fun but I felt nostalgic for the days when I heard my mom's laughter and enjoyed the smell of the turkey roasting in her oven.

Right before Christmas, I met with my plastic surgeon for the last time, but I didn't know that until I got there. We had developed a relationship and I looked forward to Dr. Bern's brief but positive critique of my healing. As he took a look at my scars, I complained about the overly pink and sore spot on my left side. He said it looked good and he cleared me for tattoos right away. I had been looking forward to no longer being medically poked and prodded, but it gave me a sense of comfort knowing that I was being checked regularly. Dr. Bern insisted it was my last appointment and I was free. *I didn't feel free. What if something went wrong?*

I had stopped in to talk to Sebastian Orth, owner of Otherworld Tattoo in Santa Barbara, before my final surgery. Sebastian was willing to help cover the scars, but wanted me to wait a minimum of nine to twelve months to let everything heal before inflicting more trauma. As eager as I was, I appreciated his conservative approach and would make my first tattoo appointment when my healing was done.

Chapter Six: Practical Suggestions

- Ask your plastic surgeon if you would benefit from liposuction.

- Ask for physical therapy sessions and get them approved by your insurance while you heal, so you are approved to start them when you are ready.

- Make an appointment with a lymphatic therapist to help aid your healing post-surgery.

- Begin light exercise as soon as your surgeon recommends. Take short walks and work your way up to longer ones. Don't over-due it.

- If you have any tender or painful spots that won't go away. Press your doctor for ideas to help healing.

- Write in a journal if you can, it helps to get your frustrations out and to help process this whole experience.

- Try to manage your stress level with meditation, massage, exercise, or another doctor approved activity. It is important to remain calm to aid in healing.

- Honor your boundaries with others and take care of yourself first.

- If you have silicone implants talk to your doctor about having them checked yearly.

Chapter Seven
Rebuilding Surprises
January 8, 2017

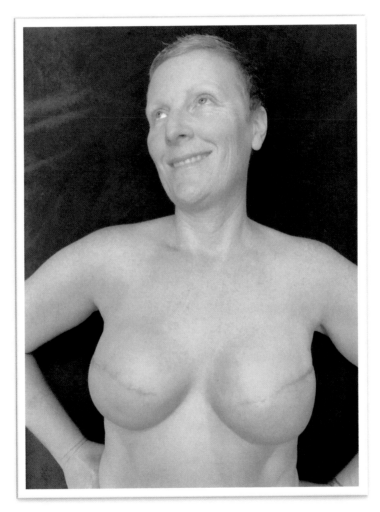

The Left breast was definitely bigger than the right...oh well.

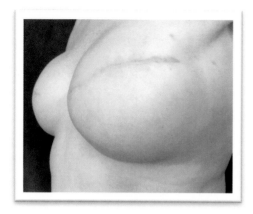 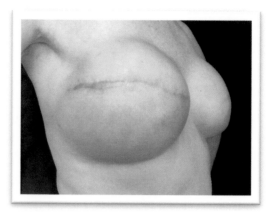

All of the breast photos Wiley took of my breasts helped me digest what had happened to me and I discovered that my left breast was bigger than my right. I kept telling myself it was probably just swelling from surgery, but after five months that really wasn't plausible. One breast bigger than the other was nothing to complain about especially since I think they had been like that before this whole nightmare. Both of my breasts had been removed along with some of the skin, both nipples, and four lymph nodes. Then the whole darn area had been rebuilt. They were the result of breast cancer and breast cancer sucked.

My friend Mercedes had been through the breast cancer process and early on in my diagnosis she had shown me her beautiful flower breast tattoos which got me dreaming about doing something similar. She also told me it took a good year for her breasts to settle. So, I sat and waited for them to settle. I felt impatient sometimes and wanted the whole process to speed up. I had always thought of myself as very patient and I truly could be when I wanted to. The ambitious, motivated side of me, wanted to move on to the next stage of my life and leave cancer in my history. I wanted my peace of mind back.

It was hard not to let a little paranoia infiltrate my mind sometimes especially since I had met other cancer survivors that were abandoned by their partners. I pondered what life would be like if Wiley had decided cancer was just way too much drama and heartache for him. *What if he had left and found a younger, perkier, fully intact set of millennial breasts to fondle?* Deep down I knew he wouldn't but I seemed to doubt everything after being diagnosed with cancer.

"You're not going to leave me, are you?" I said as Wiley buzzed around the kitchen preparing dinner. "Leave you?" He said in a surprised voice. "No. Why would I leave you? I love you, silly."

We both giggled as I took a deep breath and watched him dice vegetables and smile at me. We had been through so much and I loved him more than ever. That's one thing I could remove from my worry list. Wiley understood that cancer would be a lifetime project. He was patient and understanding and that helped. Almost twenty-three years of marriage at that time and he was still there and still my best friend. He treated me like the sexy, young, crazy twenty-one-year-old girl he fell in love with. Thank you, Wiley, you never gave up on me. With all the focus on me all the time, I was beginning to feel like I needed a new project. I was tired of all of the constant attention paid to my breasts. Every single day I imagined my breasts covered in cherry blossoms and moving on with my life.

New Issues
January 8, 2017

Diagnosed back in November of 2015, here I was in January of 2017 with a new set of issues and problems to overcome, but luckily not cancer. The latest quarterly tumor marker blood test revealed that my markers, for the third time, had dropped. That was good news. CA 15-3 protein had dropped to 12 and any number under 32 was considered normal. My no evidence of cancer that I received last July still stood. Phew. However, Dr. Shah looked closely at my breast scars and decided that I needed a dermatologist to determine what could be done about the keloid scarring that had developed. It had been five months since surgery, but the scar closest to my left underarm was very red and thick. My breast tissue had been opened during three different surgeries, stitched in the same place, and my body had to heal the same thing over and over again. In response, it had decided to over compensate by generating puffy, pink scarring and it was still tender and sore.

If that weren't enough, I had also developed axillary web syndrome (AWS) known as cording, under my breasts. The cord felt and looked like a thin vein that stuck out of my abdomen and was caused by lymphatic trauma as a result of the mastectomy. I hadn't even realized that I had cording until I stretched my arms over my head and felt a slight pulling under the skin.

Back to physical therapy where Joanna placed a heating pad on the area and informed me that the cord was not useful at all to my body, so she was going to break it. *Yikes.*

"Is that going to hurt?" I asked as I laid on the table with my left side exposed.

"I don't know, let's just go slow and see what happens" she answered.

Not sure I liked that answer, but Joanna hadn't steered me wrong yet. I trusted her and took a deep breath. She placed her thumb on the top of the cord while she rubbed downward on the middle of the cord. I started to babble on about something she probably didn't care about.

"Whoa," she said in a very surprised and slightly confused voice, "It snapped, did you feel that Holly?"

I hadn't felt anything. She rubbed around and found another cord. We originally thought there was only one but she found three. She diligently rubbed and pulled the cord with her fingers until that one snapped too. My side felt tender and bruised from the pressure of her hands. We cut our losses and made another appointment for the following week to try to eliminate the last cord. That night, I put a warm compress on my side and kept my mind off the discomfort with my usual BBC murder mysteries. I loved mysteries that had little to no active violence or blood. The worst I saw was a woman's hand draped in vintage lace and hanging off an antique chaise. Her lifeless body discovered by the maid who had entered the room to bring tea and biscuits. I was quite satisfied watching a good mystery being solved and somebody blamed for the carnage.

In the mean-time, I was walking around with Scar Away, silicone wound strips across the worst parts of the keloid scars in the hopes that it would prevent them from growing. I was also hoping they would help fade the very dark pink color. I was so sick of everything cancer related. I wanted there to be an end date to my breast cancer but there would NEVER be an end date. I loved when projects ended, so the realization that I had to monitor my tumor markers for the rest of my life was annoying. I was fourteen months out from being diagnosed and it felt like a lifetime had passed since then.

The following week, Joanna worked on the last cord but it was too deep to snap. She gave up and we decided it was not worth causing me anymore pain. Unless it got closer to the skin, she might need to just leave it alone. I was sore after that session and a little bruised too. On a positive note, I could reach my arms above my head and there was no longer a tight cord that hindered my movement. That was progress. Several weeks later when I was swimming laps at the pool I felt the last cord snap on its own.

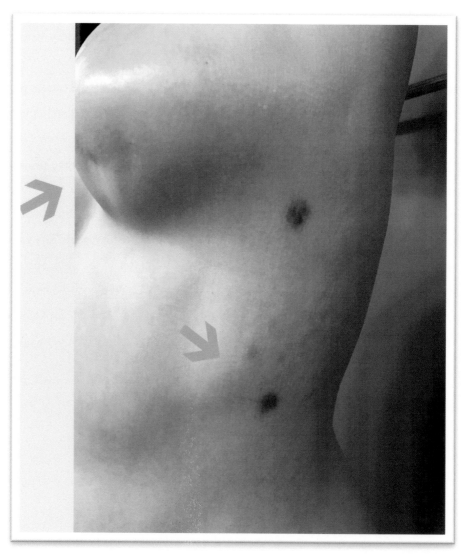

The bruises were a result of the first and second cord that were snapped. The bottom arrow shows the barely visible third cord. The top left arrow shows a new discovery, I had a dimple under my breast. I was told it was due to the lack of breast tissue and nothing to worry about. I couldn't help but laugh at my new dimple.

Can You Fix Them?
March 10, 2017

Instant gratification was not an option with breast cancer. Steady, patient determination was the only way to go. I waited several months to be approved by my insurance to consult with a dermatologist. When I finally met Dr. Robert Jordan, my first question was, "Can you do anything to make the thick, pink, keloid scars better?" Dr. Jordan put on his magnifying glasses and took a good look at my scars. He told me that they were in fact, hypertrophic scars, not keloid scars as I was originally told by several of my other doctors. He explained that keloid and hypertrophic scars are both raised scars that formed as a result of too much collagen at the site of an injury. Hypertrophic scars usually form immediately after injury while keloids can take up to a year or more to begin to form.

I shared my plans to beautify my new breasts with tattoos as soon as they were ready and explained my concern about the scarring. Lucky for me, Dr. Jordan said that he could flatten the scarring and reduce the size and color with cortisone injections over time. He promptly set up a tray and injected the scars on either side. About three to four injections were done on each side right into the scar. The left side stung a little but I felt nothing on the right side. There was a tiny amount of blood but pretty straight forward. I made a second follow up appointment for one month later. Dr. Jordan wanted to look at the healing before deciding if more injections were necessary. He explained that if too many injections were done it could actually sink the scar, so we would wait a month and then look at the results. I felt elated knowing that I was one step closer to my final tattoos.

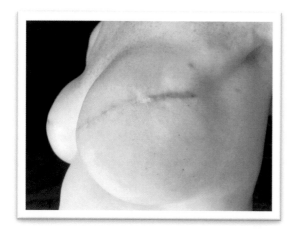 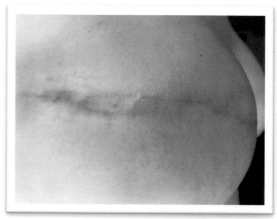

March 10, 2017: Hypertrophic scarring on both breasts, closest to my arm pits. On my right breast, you can see tiny needle marks where I was injected with cortisone for the first time.

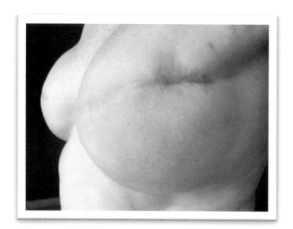 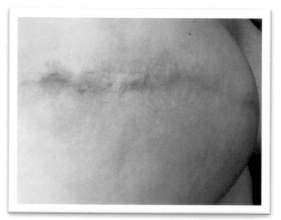

April 11, 2017: Second round of injections and the scars began to flatten out and were not as prominent.

May 25, 2017: After the third round, the scars flattened substantially and no further injections were necessary.

I'm Out of Menopause?
August 15, 2017

Right before my first tattoo session, my ovaries, which had been in chemo induced menopause for a year and a half, came back to life. *Noooooooooo.* I had been told over a year ago by my gynecologist that my hormone test numbers were a definite indicator of permanent menopause and he said, "There is no coming back from that." Imagine my surprise when I had to rush off to the store for feminine hygiene products. I experienced heavy bleeding for seven straight days which included sharp ovary pain, pelvic pain, and a shit ton of worry. My doctors became concerned with the excessive bleeding and sent me for a pelvic ultrasound.

The pelvic ultrasound done externally at first, and then internally with that horrible, dildo-like wand was done at our local hospital by their radiology department. Wiley opted to wait for me in the lobby as I warned him in advance about the awkward vaginal wand that awaited me. The results of the ultrasound showed that my endometrial lining was a tad too thick and I had an ovarian cyst on my left ovary. That was the reason for the stabbing left ovary pain I had experienced. Nobody came right out and said it but I got the feeling that there was a real possibility that I had developed a secondary cancer, either endometrial, ovarian, or uterine. I was scheduled the following week for an endometrial biopsy, "Just to be safe."

Menopause had freed me from my raging hormones, PMS, and the mood swings that came with an aging menstrual cycle, but I might be out of menopause or worse. The idea that I had possibly developed another cancer was enough to put me over the edge. The drastic upsurge of estrogen coupled with the stress transformed my usual calm self into a hurricane. Hurricane Holly violently swirled about throwing words and anger at the two people I loved the most. Wiley and Vance became the recipients of my fear as I unleashed verbally on both of them in a regrettable episode of yelling triggered by nothing of consequence. My oncologist sent me back to consult with my gynecologist and to follow up with a pelvic exam, another round of hormone testing, and an endometrial biopsy to try to figure out what was going on. I went to the gynecology consult appointment with two main questions.

- Question #1: What if I had a secondary cancer? What was the treatment?
  Answer: Depending on the cancer, a full hysterectomy would need to be done. My oncologist would be consulted to decide if chemo and/or radiation were necessary afterwards.

- Question #2: What if it was NOT cancer?
  Answer: If it was not cancer, I most likely would still need at the minimum an oophorectomy, that was the removal of both my ovaries to shut down estrogen production and put me back in the safe zone.

My gynecologist confirmed that the ovarian cyst found during the ultrasound was small and nothing to worry about. The results of a blood test I had taken to find out my menopause status included the following hormone tests:

- **FSH** (follicle-stimulating hormone) measured the amount of FSH produced by the pituitary gland which controlled the menstrual cycle and the production of eggs by the ovaries.
- **LH** (luteinizing hormone) was also produced in the pituitary gland and helped control my menstrual cycle and the production of eggs by my ovaries.
- **Estradiol** measured estrogen, the hormone made by my ovaries, breasts and adrenal glands and the hormone I was trying to avoid.[x]

All three of the tests showed elevated hormones consistent with a menstrual cycle but just to be certain I was scheduled for an endometrial biopsy. My uterine lining looked a little too thick on the ultrasound and a biopsy would hopefully provide the reason why. I had never had an endometrial biopsy before and felt slight panic about it. The procedure was done in my gynecologist's office by a nurse practitioner with decades of experience. Since I had never had one the nurse walked me through each step so there were no surprises. It turned out to be a pretty simple procedure.

Endometrial Biopsy

- A speculum was inserted into my vagina to open me up.
- A long, thin endometrial suction catheter was inserted into my vagina, through my cervix, and up into my uterus. There was slight discomfort when the probe went into my cervix.
- The probe went all the way to the back of my uterus.
- A small tissue sample was quickly removed with the probe.
- There was a quick pinch and it was over.
- The whole process took only minutes and was not that bad.

The evening after the biopsy, I had a little bit of spotting and experienced some cramping. It felt like a period. A hot pad and some ibuprofen helped the discomfort. The spotting lasted through the next day and then everything went back to normal. It took an entire excruciating week to get my biopsy results back, but they were normal. *What a relief, but at the same time, really universe?* My gynecologist and oncologist had a phone conversation about my precarious hormonal status. I was impressed when my gynecologist phoned me himself the very next day to relay the details of that dual-specialist conversation. Both of them had agreed, based on my hormone tests and high risk of occurrence, that I needed prophylactic surgery. Prophylactic means surgery done to prevent disease.

My severe reactions to Tamoxifen® and Exemestane® left me with no drug options to eliminate the high level of estrogen production in my body. The only option left was to remove my ovaries, also known as an oophorectomy. As a precaution, it was also recommended that I remove my fallopian tubes at the same time, salpingectomy. The combination of the two surgeries was known as an abdominal bilateral salpingo-oophorectomy. This was an unexpected surgery looming in my future right when I was ready to move on. I envisioned an advertising campaign with me at the center, smiling with no shirt on, and the tagline "Breast cancer, the gift that keeps on giving."

Wiley and I met with my new surgeon, Dr. Gustafson, the following week and got the details of the pending procedure. My number one question didn't relate to the surgery at all as I had spent copious amounts of time googling the procedure. I really wanted to know if the surgery was going to postpone my breast tattoos. Yes, at that point, I was obsessed with them being completed. Dr. Gustafson laughed and admitted that in his multi-decade career he had never been asked about tattoos and surgery. I told him that my tattoo artist had wanted me to wait at least two weeks in between surgery and tattooing, so that I was not healing from two things at once. Dr. Gustafson thought that seemed practical. I planned to postpone my tattoo appointments for one month to rest and recover.

Ovaries Be Gone!
October 10, 2017

It would be my fourth major surgery in less than two years and there were risks with every procedure. I know it was morbid but before each surgery, I spoke with Wiley about the worst-case-scenario.

"If I don't make it home alive, there is plenty of life insurance for you to stay in our current house or you and Vance could relocate back to Santa Barbara if you wanted to?" I said rather matter of fact.

I hadn't noticed the tears rolling down Wiley's cheeks until we both burst into laughter and I assured him I would be coming home. Death isn't a topic for the faint of heart and we usually tackled it with a good sense of humor. We ran through the list of women that would NOT make good suitors for Wiley if he were widowed. We hugged, laughed and moved on with our day.

That night Wiley said, "Holly, no matter what happens, I will make sure your book gets finished." I hadn't even thought about that. I contemplated leaving Wiley and Vance final notes but I knew I would be coming home. I had too much to live for and too much to do. It was not my time yet because my book needed to be finished and so did my tattoos.

Vance was almost seventeen-years-old and he got himself up and drove to school in my car the morning of my surgery. I peeked out the garage door as Vance pulled away from our house with a mixture of emotions. I was proud that he had become a responsible, young man but longed for the days we cuddled and giggled while playing with his favorite toys on the living room floor. I knew that he would be alright if the surgery took my life but desperately hoped I had many more years with him.

Abdominal bilateral salpingo-oophorectomy. *How in the world am I supposed to remember what it's called?* I took Latin in seventh grade but I was pretty sure it didn't include that kind of complexity. "Estella est in atrio", (Estella is in the hallway) and "Canis est in atrio" (The dog is in the hallway) were the only two phrases that I retained from Latin class. *Why was Estella, the matron of the house and the dog in the hallway?* Nurses whirled around my hospital bed and all I could think about was Estella and her dog and how I wished I was in the hallway with them and not about to be wheeled into an operating room, again.

I was the last scheduled surgery of the day at the Same Day Surgery center and expected quite a wait to be rolled into the operating room. Two o'clock in the afternoon was not ideal for surgery as I had been fasting since the night before. I missed breakfast and lunch but it was the only day and time Dr. Gustafson had available in his busy schedule before December, so I took it. Thirty minutes after checking into the surgery center I was already prepped and ready for surgery. A nurse brought Wiley back and let us both know I would be going in early. *Sweet!* Dr. Gustafson stopped by for a quick chat and then my anesthesiologist stopped by to talk about all of my drug sensitivities and his sedation plan. There was no one else waiting for surgery, so I had everyone's focus.

Wiley leaned in for one last kiss as the anesthesiologist pulled a needle out of my IV and Wiley's smile began to fade out of my vision as I announced that the first margarita was great and then my eyes closed. I was wheeled in at one o'clock, a full hour before I was scheduled. Around four o'clock I remember Wiley holding my hand and smiling as my eyelids opened again and I became aware of my surroundings in recovery. The nurse told me that surgery went well and I was ready to go home. They gave me an IV cocktail of some sort before they discharged me that would make the half hour drive from Ventura to Ojai more pleasant. Wiley helped me dress and I was whisked to my car in a wheelchair. I had checked in to the surgery center at noon and by five o'clock I was safely tucked into my own bed at home ready for a snooze. *Pretty incredible!*

Dr. Gustafson had told me at my pre-op appointment that after the surgery "It will hurt like hell." I appreciated the honesty but maybe it was too honest. He also described the procedure as, "A major surgery, done through small incisions." *Oh boy!*

Before anything was removed, my abdomen was expanded using carbon dioxide (C02) gas which gave the surgeon more space to safely work. The surgery was done laparoscopically, which meant Dr. Gustafson had made three small incisions in my abdomen. The first incision was done through my belly button where a tube with a light and camera were inserted. The camera carefully guided him when he removed my parts. The other two incisions were on either side of my abdomen, above my pelvic bone and below my belly button.

In my pre-op-appointment I asked how he would remove my parts and he was more than willing to explain, as most patients wanted far less details. Dr. Gustafson told me he would first look around to make sure that my ovaries and fallopian tubes were easily accessible. If he couldn't access them easily, a much larger abdominal incision would have to be made so that he did not damage the surrounding tissue and organs. A pouch would be placed over each ovary and the ovary would be cut out of my body. The pouch would carefully be pulled out of the incision right above it with the ovary tucked inside.

When I asked about my fallopian tube removal, he told me that each fallopian tube was like a gummy worm; soft, flexible, and gummy in texture. He said the fallopian tubes would easily be removed. *Pretty sure I will never be able to eat or look at a gummy worm candy the same again.* Due to my allergy to medical adhesive, he would not be using any medical glue to avoid possible reactions and would suture the incisions instead. Lucky for me, my parts cooperated and were right where they needed to be for removal.

My belly was distended from the carbon dioxide gas and Dr. Gustafson warned me that many patients experienced back and neck pain on the left side as a result of the gas being trapped in the body. As a preventive measure, when I was wheeled into recovery, I was put on 100% oxygen for ten minutes. The CO_2 gas would bind with the pure oxygen and I would breath it out. My surgeons handy trick prevented me from experiencing any CO_2 pain during recovery.

For the next few days, I binge watched British TV shows via Netflix and Amazon Prime while I tried to keep my eyelids from closing under the weight of the prescription codeine. I took my codeine prescription every four hours setting alarms in the middle of the night for the first twenty-four hours, then I tapered off, taking one pill every five hours and then every six hours and so on. My surgery was Tuesday afternoon and by Friday morning, I was off the opioid medication completely. I experienced another round of constipation thanks to the pain pills. Thankfully, it was alleviated after several prune juice-Metamucil cocktails and a stool softener, lovingly prepared, served with a smile and a giggle by Nurse Wiley.

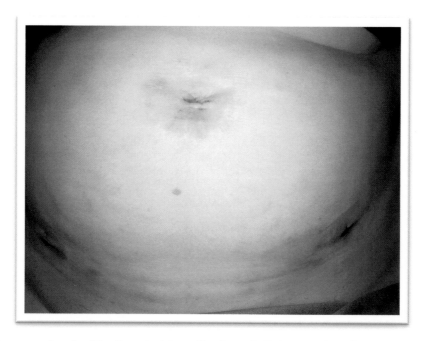

Light bruising around each of the three incisions. One in my belly button, the other two over my ovaries. My abdomen was distended and swollen for about a week while healing. It was like being pregnant again.

I felt very bloated and had to be careful with leaning over and twisting my abdomen due to the many layers of sutures holding my incisions closed. I was instructed to not lift anything over ten pounds for a whole month. My abdomen ached, but I got relief when I used a microwaveable hot pad on my stomach. The discomfort was not unbearable and I relaxed on the couch and Wiley took care of me. By the second week my abdomen was less painful and I felt more like myself.

144

Chapter Seven: Practical Suggestions

- Have you had your hormones checked? It might be a good idea to ask your doctor. It is a simple blood test and could give you an idea of where you are in relation to menopause.
- Ask your doctor if you will need any prophylactic (preventive) surgeries to reduce your cancer risk. Examples include ovary removal, hysterectomy, etc....
- When unexpected problems arise, ask lots of questions for all possible scenarios. Do not assume that your doctor will give you all of the information. You have to be your own advocate all the time.
- If you are having laparoscopic surgery, ask your surgeon if they will put you on 100% oxygen for ten minutes while in recovery. According to my surgeon, it will help with the CO_2 discomfort post-surgery.
- Seek out specialists to help with unusual symptoms or to relieve pain and discomfort. If you notice anything new in your body, question your doctors about it. Don't accept pain or discomfort as normal. Ask if there is a way to relieve your symptoms with physical therapy, exercise, or specialized medical treatments.
- Continue physical therapy until you feel like you have your full range of motion back. Your body has been through a lot and you may be experiencing pain in your arms, back, neck or other areas that will benefit from therapy.
- How are your scars healing? Do you still have sensitivity after six months or more? Are your scars very puffy and red? If your scars bother you, ask to see a dermatologist to help reduce the look of your scars and also any residual symptoms post-surgery.
- How are you feeling about where you are in this process? Do you need more support? If that's a yes, attend a breast cancer support group in your area. Ask your oncologist or check with your local cancer center for resources.
- Be gentle with yourself. Try not to judge your body for all of its new flaws. Work on accepting the new you with all of your scars and imperfections. Talk about it with someone if you are having a tough time.
- Do things that you love. Enjoy every minute that you have. What have you been putting off? Make plans, meet with friends and family, and reconnect to your old life.

Chapter Eight
My Final Chapter...Ink
August 30, 2017

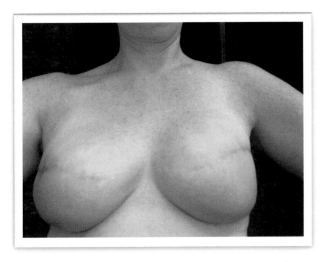

The night before my first tattoo session. It had been one whole year since my breast implant surgery and the cortisone shots had flattened my scars as much as possible. It was time for tattoos.

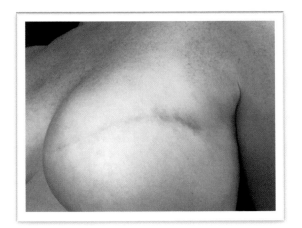

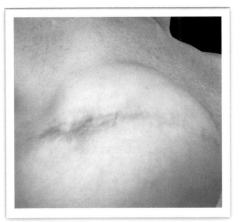

In Japan, cherry blossoms are the symbols of Spring, renewal, and the impermanence of life. The blossoms start to fall just two short weeks after they bloom. I didn't know their meaning when I chose them but it seems very fitting in hindsight. Wiley had shown me photos of tattoos that included scars, instead of trying to cover them up with ink. That idea resonated with me and I realized that the thick, red scars could be used as the base for the cherry blossom tree branches. Sebastian had told me that puffy pink scars tend to suck up a lot of ink, so Wiley's idea would solve that problem. He was glad I had waited a full year to allow my breasts to heal.

The day of the appointment Sebastian had a drawing ready for me and the design was perfect. He did not transfer the design onto my breast using tattoo paper. Instead, he used colored Sharpie pens to draw the design free-hand directly on my skin. That gave him the ability to customize the location of my tattoo based on my scars and shape of my breasts. I had originally wanted a cluster of cherry blossoms where my nipples used to be but Sebastian pointed out it was way too obvious. He was right. So, the blossoms were placed a little off center.

The first session was three and a half hours long and resulted in a full outline on my left breast. I was surprised by the lack of pain involved in the outlining. I had other tattoos and remembered it being extremely painful. With the lack of nerve endings and no nipples, the needle stung across my skin but never created the kind of lip-biting, wince-inducing pain I remembered. The sensation of a light sunburn and nothing more. It went very fast as Sebastian and I chatted about life.

When he was done wiping the blood and plasma off my freshly inked skin, I went to the mirror for the long-awaited results. I loved how the branch organically arched its way up my side and onto my left breast using the scar as part of the branch. I opted to be aggressive with my tattoo timeline. The next session would be two weeks away and if I kept this up they would be completed before my two-year diagnosis anniversary in November.

 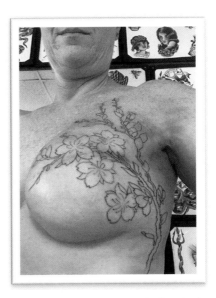

Sharpie drawing on the left to use as a guide. Final tattooed outline on the right, ready for shading and color.

Ink Me Again!
September 13, 2017

The second tattoo session took four hours and the outlining was annoying but not incredibly painful. Sebastian and I chatted for a while and then I closed my eyes and zoned out while his music played in the background. The shading added a new dimension to the tattoo and pain. Having multiple needles shade over and over on the same sensitive skin definitely hurt more than the outline. Every once in a while, he would hit a spot that sent a more powerful zing through the skin and caused my nerves to react. Compared to the insane pain after my double mastectomy, the pain from tattooing felt like no big deal and the final result would be totally worth it.

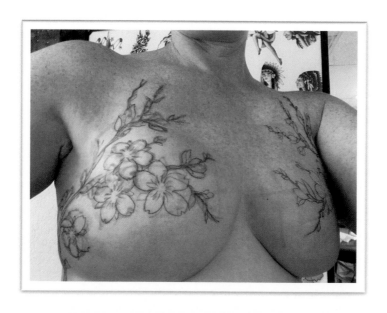

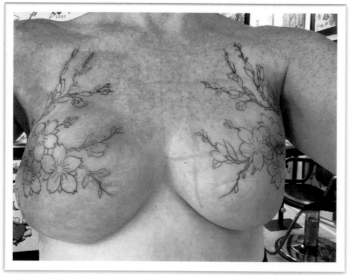

. The branches from the cherry blossom tree flowed organically across each breast, similar but not the same. Sebastian completed both outlines, so, we had time to begin the shading on my left breast.

150

He colored in the branches and then started shading the leaves, flowers, and outside the outline, which gave it dimension. When he eventually added color, the back shading would make the design pop.

A Pretty Shade of Pink
September 27, 2017

I was over the moon with my tattoo progress. I felt like I had reclaimed my breasts. Cancer had taken so much from me but I was making them mine again. With the outlines and the shading done on the left breast, it was time to shade the right breast and start adding color. The third session took five full hours and the results took my breath away. Looking in the mirror, the scars and the absence of my nipples were no longer the focus of my breasts. Instead, beautiful, pink, cherry blossoms exuded hope.

The question most people asked when they saw my tattoos was "Does it hurt?" YES! Tattoos definitely hurt. Some areas on my breast were a lot more sensitive than others. It hurt a lot down the side of my body where the branches originated. The top of my chest where the branches end was also very sensitive. The least sensitive area was the skin that ran along the lines of both breast scars. That area had no feeling since I finished the third breast surgery and I didn't anticipate the feeling would ever come back. Everyone has a different pain tolerance and I think I have a very high tolerance for pain after experiencing natural child birth with Vance and all of the incredibly painful breast surgeries. I hoped that I would never experience anything similar to the pain that was generated as a result of the double mastectomy. That was excruciating.

I had gone alone to the first three tattoo sessions, but the last tattoo session was scheduled in November on a Sunday, a day Wiley and I usually spent together. Wiley had expressed the desire for a Japanese style upper arm tattoo that would incorporate some cherry blossoms in it too. I thought it would make the best Christmas gift, so before I left my third session, I made an appointment for Wiley as a surprise.

The outlines and shading were done on both sides, so Sebastian started adding color to the right breast. After tattooing, it was normal for the skin to be red and tender and the colors to appear darker for a week or more as it healed. It usually took about two weeks for the tattoo to fully heal.

Final Tattoo Session
November 12, 2017

It was finally time for my final tattoo session and I wanted Wiley to be there for the finish. He had run the marathon right alongside me for 24 months, handing me water, cheering me on, and carrying me across the finish-line. The race was over and we could both sit down to rest. I also wanted Wiley there to document my final progress with photos and video to share with you.

The vision I had held for two years was happening. I was so grateful to Sebastian for providing a safe, relaxed, and private space for me to be transformed. At my last session, I stared at the shop ceiling for the last time. The sound of the tattoo machine buzzed over an eclectic mix of retro blues and punk tunes. Sebastian carefully filled the branches, leaves, and flowers of my design with color. He brought the tattoos to life and my two-year long nightmare to an end.

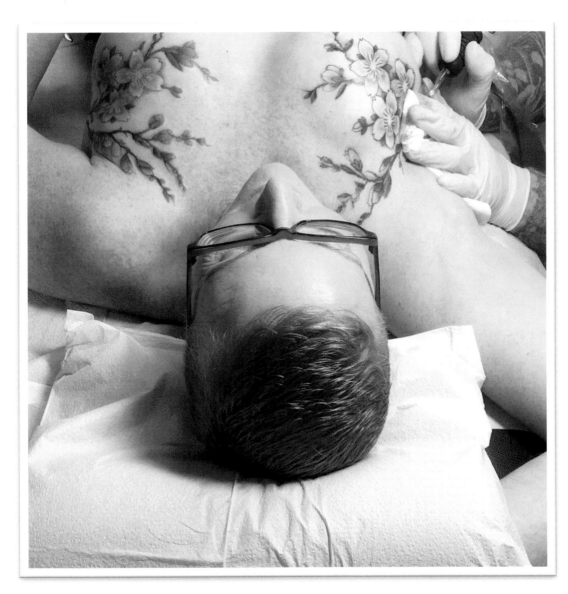

Photo by Catherine Masi

Photo by Catherine Masi

156

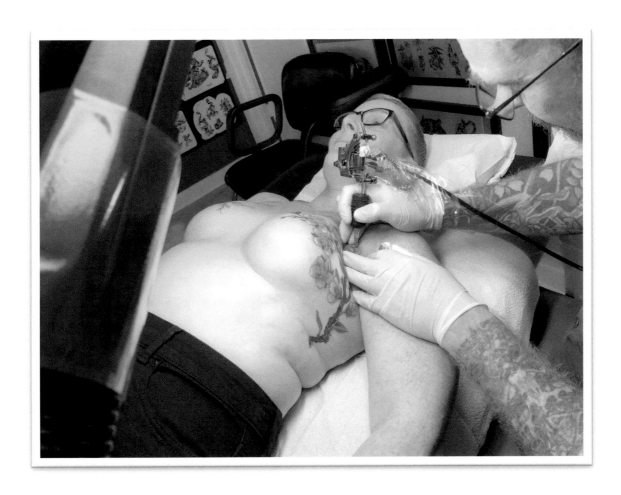

A final five-hour session and my breast cancer scars were covered with the most beautiful cherry blossoms. The scars were not gone, just reinvented. I loved them. They were better than I had imagined. Sebastian had Catherine Masi, his friend and shop photographer, document my last session. Catherine was so supportive and I will never forget her crying as we talked about this journey coming to an end.

Full Bloom
November 2017

I had come full circle in exactly two years. That was quick. I know women that have dealt with their cancer for years, some for decades. I felt grateful that my journey had come to an end. I was able to get off the roller coaster but I would be hanging around the theme park for the rest of my life. I wanted to share my story to demystify breast cancer treatment and also to let women know that they can do it.

If you or someone you know has breast cancer, I know that you probably want to see the backside of everyone and everything cancer related but you might not be able to do that completely. So, gear up for that reality and make the best of it. I like to think of my quarterly oncology appointments as preventive care. I still dread the results of my tumor marker tests because my mind creeps back to the idea that it could come back, but I have trained myself to stay optimistic and not go to the dark place.

Breast cancer has ignited a desire to share my story with others. To write, speak, and comfort women experiencing this painful and traumatizing disease. Cancer is not always a death sentence but something in you does die. The trick is finding something new in your life to be passionate about. It doesn't have to be cancer related. It just needs to feed your soul and put your mind and body at peace. I know that is a tall order, you have been through so much. You have endured the heartache, loss, stress, discomfort, mental anguish, and physical pain that cancer brings. You still might have more ahead of you and I might too. Each woman's cancer experience is unique like her.

I know that calling it a journey in a way is romanticizing it and there is nothing romantic about cancer, but I need to call it a journey because journeys always end. My breast cancer was more like an unexpected detour down a road I had never been on. It was fraught with all kinds of drama and peril but a journey none the less. You can call it what you like. No matter where you are in the process, you have to try to make peace with it and deal with it the best you can.

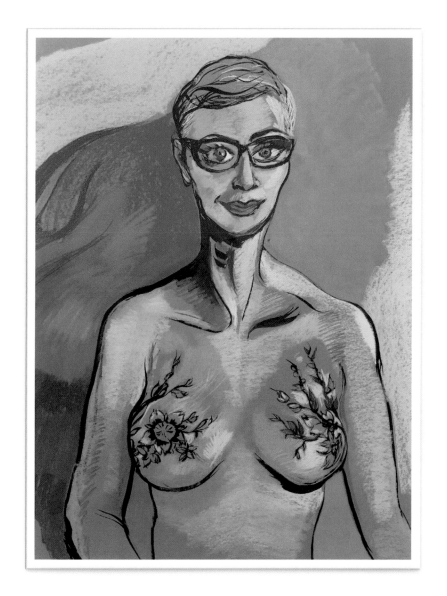

After my tattoos were healed, I sat for a portrait by my friend and artist, Vera Long. I love the brilliant, unrestrained color, and vitality portrayed in her art. I knew my portrait would be the cover of my book.

What I am asking you to do is take time for you. Reclaim who you are now. You are most likely not the same person you were before you were diagnosed with cancer. I know I'm not. Start asking yourself important questions to get YOU back.

- What brings me joy?
- What do I want to do with my time and my life now?
- Am I happy in my career or do I need to change it?
- What have I always wanted to do but put on the back burner?

Put aside the cost and all of the things holding you back. Now ask yourself, what should I be doing right now? No, not your laundry. Really, take some quiet time to reflect inward and search your soul to answer this question. This is the time to reinvent YOU. You are alive right now. There is no guarantee that you have any more time in your future. You might want or feel you deserve more, you do, but cancer is brutal and it does not care what you want. It has its own agenda. Our time here is limited and that goes for everyone here, even those never diagnosed with cancer. You and I cannot predict the remainder of your life and what that looks like. This is the time for action.

You need to take a deep breath and gently push yourself forward out of the darkness and back into the light. Sit in the sun and feel the warmth, the love, the endless possibilities. It feels so good to do it. Reclaim who you are and who you want to be. Cancer does not have to define you and your future. The sky is the limit. Make it happen. You are powerful, loved, and needed by others. Get out there and make your dreams come true. Plant your new dream and let it bloom.

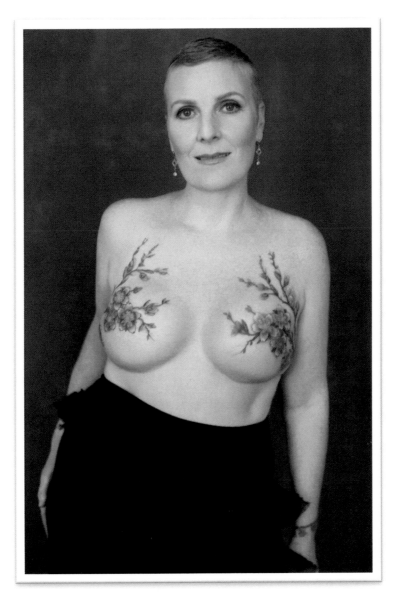

Photo by Ashleigh Taylor Portrait

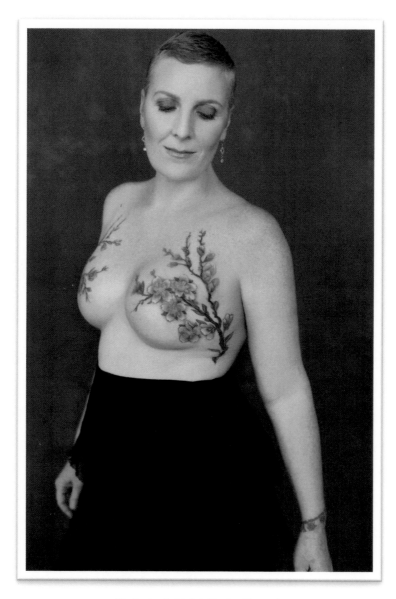

Photo by Ashleigh Taylor Portrait

Photo by Ashleigh Taylor Portrait

After such a harrowing breast cancer experience, I wanted to have professional photos taken of Wiley and I for the book and for us. I wanted to show other women that breast cancer and reconstruction are beautiful. Ashleigh Taylor provided the full glamour shoot experience with hair, make-up, and gorgeous clothing in her private downtown Santa Barbara studio. She played our favorite 1980's tunes which made the shoot fun and also relaxed both of us. We felt really comfortable which allowed her to capture who we are in the photos. We love this tender photo that incorporates both of our tattoos, our wedding rings, and our commitment to each other. We hadn't had professional photos of us as a couple since our wedding photos in 1994. Thank you, Ashleigh, for these gorgeous photos that document this time in our lives.

Acknowledgements

I am deeply grateful for the assistance, encouragement, and support from the following people. My doctors; Dr. Samuel Bern, Dr. John C. Gustafson, Dr. Robert R. Jordan, Dr. Constanze S. Rayhrer, and Dr. Shilpa Shah. My lymphatic therapist, Alicia Morris and physical therapist, Joanna Schindel. Zhena Muzyka for providing a safe and encouraging space for my book to blossom in both her Empowered Author's Academy and Writing Mastermind. My fellow memoir Mastermind writers that listened, shared, and supported me; Carol Marshall, Kathy Davenport, Kristen Smith, and Ixchel Leigh. Rosalie Zabilla for being present every step of my cancer journey, you are my best friend. Maureen O'Brien, your unwavering enthusiasm and supportive editing gave me the confidence to self-publish this book. To my Kingston's Candy Girls (adopted daughters without all of the paperwork) you have brought so much to my life; Chelsi Caspersen, Hannah Cody, Jordan Heath, Alexis Chahivec, and Lucia Zabilla. My countless friends; Martina Albert, Mercedes Gallup, Kathy Hartley, Risa Horowitz, Sam Horowitz, Jeffrey Horton, Kathleen Horton, Nicole Jones, Susan Kapadia, Vera Long, Renee Mandala, Bruce McFadden, Suzanne McKenna, Danna Tartaglia-Orr, Pamela Robins (for coming up with my book title, *Bittersweet*, in your dream), David Tate, Sage Tate, Jon Valois, and the ladies of the Ojai Valley Woman's Club. Sebastian Orth at Otherworld Tattoo for transforming my cancer scars into works of art. Catherine Masi for documenting the final tattoo appointment with photos. Ashleigh Taylor your photos of Wiley and I are exquisite and we will cherish them. My parents, John and Carol Bishop, loved to listen to our stories and encouraged us to be ourselves, you are missed every single day. My sisters, June K. Martin and Sarah K. Jaimes; Mom and Dad would be so proud of us and I love you. Grandma Rita for always encouraging my creativity and for sharing your own writing when we were growing up. I wish you were here, because I know that you would be tickled with your granddaughter being a published author. My cousin, Carolynne Holston, and my Aunt, Susan Holston, have lovingly listened, supported, and given me great advice. My mother-in-law, Karen Thrasher, for her constant love and support. My biggest supporter and partner in life, Wiley D. Thrasher, I love being married to you. Finally, I want to thank my most loving critic and son, Vance K. Thrasher. You are the reason I get out of bed every morning. Thank you for your detailed editing skills and thoughtful ideas for the book. I love you.

Continuing the Story
Engage with me at:

HollyKThrasher.com

Facebook: HollyKThrasher

Instagram: @HollyKThrasher

Twitter: @HollyKThrasher

Youtube: HollyKThrasher

Endnotes

[i] https://www.webmd.com/cancer/cancer-stages#1

[ii] http://breastcancernow.org/about-breast-cancer/have-you-recently-been-diagnosed-with-breast-cancer/understanding-your-results/grades-and-stages

[iii] https://www.cancer.net/research-and-advocacy/asco-care-and-treatment-recommendations-patients/white-blood-cell-growth-factors

[iv] https://dammitdolls.com/Home

[v] https://www.cancer.net/about-us/collaborations/top-five-list-oncology/choosing-wisely%C2%AE-top-five-cancer-related-tests-procedures-and-treatments-many-patients-do-not-need/topic-4-follow-tumor-marker-tests-and-imaging-tests-people-treated-breast-cancer

[vi] https://www.cancer.net/survivorship/long-term-side-effects-cancer-treatment

[vii] https://www.breastcancer.org/treatment/hormonal/serms

[viii] https://www.mayoclinic.org/drugs-supplements/tamoxifen-oral-route/side-effects/drg-20066208

[ix] https://www.breastcancer.org/research-news/ais-up-heart-problem-risk

[x] https://www.healthline.com/health/menopause/tests-diagnosis